THE TIDDLY QUID
AND AFTER

THE TIDDLY QUID AND AFTER

*A Memoir of People and Places
Met on the Way*

Nicholas Gordon Lennox

Book Guild Publishing
Sussex, England

First published in Great Britain in 2006 by
The Book Guild Ltd
Pavilion View
19 New Road
Brighton, East Sussex
BN1 1UF

Typesetting in Times by
Keyboard Services, Luton, Bedfordshire

Printed in Great Britain by
CPI Bath

A catalogue record for this book is available from
The British Library

ISBN 1 85776 921 X

This book is dedicated to my wife, Mary, who reminded me of many facts, set them in order and generally gave cohesion where none existed before. She was patient with my silences and my moments of impatience. She wrote many letters herself about our lives at home and abroad. They are fluent and amusing, and I hope one day she will incorporate them in a book of her own.

CONTENTS

NOTE

The writing of this book provided Nicky with a welcome distraction throughout the last two difficult years of his life.

The family would like to thank Kenneth Rose for his patient help in reading the proofs.

MGL

INTRODUCTION

This book is not an autobiography, nor a diplomatic memoir, nor a travel book, nor a narrative of events. It is a jumble of bits of my life, with some curious things that happened on the way.

ACKNOWLEDGEMENTS

Most of the stories in this book depend on family folk memory and my own, which for reasons I do not really understand remains surprisingly good. Several people in particular deserve my especial thanks. One is Libby Heathcote, who used to be a Dame at B.P. Gailey's House (which the young princes, William and Harry, attended) at Eton, and who lives, happily for us, in Chichester. The others are helpers at home, nurses or trainee nurses, to whom I am grateful for their technical ability and a patience with drudgery. I would also like to thank the Archives Department at the super-efficient West Sussex County Council. My thanks also to Rosemary Baird, the archivist at Goodwood, a writer and researcher of great ability who put me right on many points of editing, detail and fact.

1

War and the Atlantic

Goodwood House is a curious-looking building dating mainly from the Regency period, when long wings were added to a small hunting box with Georgian extensions. Its present shape is a three-sided building with four round towers at the corners crowned with copper domes which have turned green over the years. It seems to have followed a design by the Third Duke of Richmond (the great-grandson of Charles II and his mistress Louise de Kerouaille), in collaboration with James Wyatt, the fashionable architect of the period. A slightly older building, the stables – the work of Sir William Chambers – stands just to one side of it. It is a large handsome building of flint, stone and red brick. When the horse races take place at Goodwood every year (now 21 days' racing), it still houses horses and jockeys.

The family which lived there when I went there in 1935 at the age of four consisted of my parents, my elder brother Charles, and our nanny, Helen Hay. Helen was the daughter of the head gardener at Alnwick, whose owner, our cousin the Duke of Northumberland, declared that Helen, who had been his nursery maid, was the only woman he had ever really loved in his life. There were, of course, other servants in the house. Indeed, in the past hundred years the house must have changed very little. Since 1928, my grandfather, who had been in a wheelchair from 1916 (from polio contracted on his journey with the army to Gallipoli in

1

World War I), lived at Molecomb, the dower house at Goodwood. From 1903 his father, a lonely widower, lived at the big house with his two daughters from his second marriage to look after him. When he died in 1928, my grandparents moved to Goodwood and in turn left it to my own parents when my grandfather himself died in 1935. My father was not brought up to be a duke. He had an elder brother in the Irish Guards, who had been a prisoner of war in 1918, and at the war's end had rejoined the army with a force in support of the White Russians at Archangel, fighting with a British force against the Bolsheviks. He was a great friend of the future Queen Elizabeth the Queen Mother, who often stayed at Molecomb before her marriage to the Duke of York. My uncle was killed by a sniper near Archangel in 1920, aged only 19.

It was a happy house, tranquil with a jolly atmosphere. It seemed always filled with flowers, especially arum lilies, the speciality of our head gardener, Mr Capon, who regularly sent them to Covent Garden. In the mornings, another wonderful smell was the aroma of coffee made for the grown-ups' breakfast, with little bowls of coffee sugar from which my brother and I helped ourselves when no one was looking. The silence was tangible, with the only noises being the very occasional aircraft sound from the nearby RAF airfield at Tangmere and sometimes the roar of the engines from one of my father's cars. He was one of the most successful racing drivers of his time. He gave it up in 1930 (aged 26), just before I was born, having won many races, notably the prestigious 'Double Twelve' at Brooklands. Another noise was the wheelbarrow of logs which Freddie Phillips, the odd-job man, delivered daily to the 'porter's lodge' up an uneven stone path leading to the back door above which Charles and I slept. Some time later it was learnt that Freddie Phillips had died. My mother sent a wreath for the funeral. The next day she looked in at

Freddie's cottage on her way up to London. She found Freddie sitting up in bed, very cheerful. The wreath, with which he was delighted, was hung on the end of his bedstead with a message of affectionate condolence attached to it.

The noise which I remember most at Goodwood was that of the rooks chatting to each other and roosting in the higher branches of the beech trees to the south of the house. The rookery there is one of the biggest in England. There was always a dog with us – first, my mother's Scottie, Ethel, then a large black poodle, Bruno. The latter had a friend who belonged to the housekeeper. When they had finished playing in the garden, Bruno entered the house by the front door, his friend returning to the back door: a neat and accepted piece of class distinction. He liked sweets very much but was a late developer in barking. It was only when my mother mentioned the name Charbonnel and Walker, an extremely expensive chocolate shop in London, that Bruno was moved to bark, loudly but only once. He enjoyed swimming, and we would sometimes find him diving into the swimming pool behind Goodwood House all by himself. In front of the house, two ancient and long-retired employees, Abbot and McCarthy, raked and weeded the gravel. 'Here we be, Your Grace,' they said to my father at about this time, 'scratching about like two old fowl.'

In the 1940s Goodwood House became a hospital for servicemen retreating from the German advance into France. Goodwood is a very large house. Indeed, in those days it could sleep something near a hundred people. The grandest rooms were turned into hospital wards for the wounded, who arrived in great numbers, and after its transformation into a hospital we were left with only four rooms for our family. My brother and I played endlessly together, there being few other little boys of our age and background in the area. My mother had a resident ladies' maid, Miss Clarke, and there was a housekeeper/cook, Mrs Stacey, of whom more later. Before the war, there must have been nearly 20 servants in the house, many of whom had joined the forces or left either in or around 1939 to do other war-related work. My father sensibly decided that in the circumstances there was no point in us staying there. We left the house, my brother and I being placed at Ludgrove, the fashionable preparatory school, at the ages of nine and eleven respectively. My father, a technical near genius, gained us great kudos by landing his own aeroplane, a German 1930s Klemm, with two open cockpits, on Ludgrove football field. It was safe and solid, and its cruising speed was 90 miles per hour. A little later, midway through my second term at school, my parents came to see us with a picnic and told us we would shortly be leaving for Canada. My chief memory of the time, however, is of eating many Crunchie bars, the formula for which seems happily not to have changed since then. The thinking behind the move was that Goodwood, which is about 15 minutes from the coast, was on a very likely invasion route for an invading German army and altogether too close to a number of active RAF airfields, and thus not the place for a young family to be living at that particular moment. We – Charles, my Aunt Molly, to whom we were very close, and I – were therefore to sail from Liverpool to Montreal in the next few days to spend some time (perhaps even the entire duration of the war) there.

Our trip across the Atlantic to Canada took place just before the Battle of Britain. The plan had a local origin. A house called Stansted was the nearest stately home to Goodwood, and this was owned by an old gentleman called Lord Bessborough. He had a small son called George, who was a friend of mine, but more important, Lord Bessborough had much earlier been Governor General of Canada and had many contacts there. He had collected together a group of children, mainly relatives and friends, and made arrangements for them to be taken to Canada and lodged for the duration of the war with an old and extremely rich friend of his called John McConnell. I suppose there were two dozen or so of us, who were accordingly removed from our schools, went by train to Liverpool and thence by sea to Montreal. There were only a few adults on board, one of them being my Aunt Molly, who was in charge of Charles and me, but with a certain moral authority over a wider group of us. There was also another lady, Emily, Lady Bessborough's personal maid, who had a squint and rather frightened us, although I am told she had a heart of gold.

It took about two weeks to cross the Atlantic, and we must have been exposed to considerable danger which none of us realised at the time. The ship was a medium-sized liner belonging to the Canadian Pacific Company called the *Duchess of Bedford*. Its passenger list reveals it to have been very crowded. There were many children on board, some very small, presumably with the same objective as ourselves and quite a number of adults, mainly of Canadian, American or other nationalities, leaving England for their respective homes. It was certainly exciting. When we left London, my father was deeply sad at our departure. My mother later told me he did not speak on his way home from King's Cross Station to Norfolk Crescent, W2, where we lived. I suspect he thought he would never see us again.

My brother and I, however, recollect no moment when we were afraid or apprehensive; we were just excited. The three of us shared a cabin – my aunt and brother had beds, and I had a little bunk bed on top of my brother's. He and I had a great row about who should have the bunk bed, a row that was repeated many times on our later travels. I had two books with me – Herbert Strang's *Historical Omnibus*, a collection of adventure stories based vaguely at the time of Robin Hood, and another called *100 Best Jokes*, which I read aloud to my long-suffering brother and aunt when I

5

thought they needed cheering up. How I must have bored them!

What we did not know until much later was that the liner which left Liverpool only days after we did – the *Arandora Star* – following the same route as ourselves was torpedoed and sank with many lives lost. Its passengers were not, as rumour had it at the time, evacuated children like us, but aliens living in Britain, who the British Government thought were undesirable and a possible threat to security, and whom Canada had agreed to accept. It turned out that many of these were Italian, some said to be particularly dangerous. But many seemed in retrospect to be quite harmless; others were respectable people who had lived and worked in Britain for a long time, for example as waiters and waitresses at hotels and restaurants. I am told that, in London, people complained at the drop in standards of efficiency at the Savoy. Some were saved, but a lot drowned. There was, later on, a formal enquiry into who the passengers were, and how and why they had been selected at the last minute for this evacuation. We in the *Duchess of Bedford*, a few days ahead and cut off from the world, were mercifully ignorant of all these events.

With hindsight, we were lucky to have escaped unscathed. A little later on, on September 17th, another transatlantic liner called the *City of Benares* was torpedoed 600 miles from land while on more or less the same route as ourselves to Canada. It had separated from the convoy with which it was travelling. The *City of Benares* carried about 400 people, half passengers and half crew. Among the passengers were 90 children and 9 escorts, travelling under a government-sponsored children's overseas reception scheme. There was lifeboat accommodation for all, passengers and crew. In mid-Atlantic, there was a heavy swell and a strong wind, and the ship was stuck by a German torpedo. The wind increased to a gale, and it was impossible to lower all the lifeboats. The next day 113 survivors were picked up from the sea by a warship, including 13 children and 18 women. Subsequently another 46 survivors were rescued from a lifeboat, and of these 6 were children and 2 were adults escorting them under the government scheme. Another liner, the *City of Simla*, was torpedoed four days later on the same route. It was to have carried 30 children under the government-sponsored scheme, but these were withdrawn after news reached England of the sinking of the *City of Benares*. The formal report on these disasters recommended that the government-sponsored scheme for evacuation of children to the Dominions should be abandoned; the children would be far less at risk in rural England, even if there were an invasion, than running the gauntlet of U-boats in the Atlantic.

Our ship was very crowded. We nevertheless found space to play with the other children on the upper deck and felt rather seasick a lot of the time. The big drama was in the middle of one night when our ship shuddered with a shattering bang and seemed likely to capsize. All the lights went out and we were summoned to our lifeboat stations with our life-jackets on. Most of the adults were deeply concerned, but the children hardly at all. It turned out that a sudden strong wind had been the cause of a freak wave, which the adults had felt certain was a torpedo from one of the German U-boats patrolling the area.

Eventually we sighted land, the large low-lying island of Anticosti at the mouth of the St Lawrence River. Sailing past Quebec a day or two later, with a view of its cathedral, we were reminded of my ancestor, the Fourth Duke of Richmond, who was buried there. He had been Governor of Upper Canada, and it was his wife who had given the famous ball in Brussels on the eve of the battle of Waterloo. We docked at Montreal in glorious weather and were met by members of the McConnell family.

Mr McConnell was a courteous and kindly gentleman in his sixties with snow-white hair. He owned the biggest sugar refinery in Canada as well as the best-selling newspaper, *The Montreal Daily Star*, and other prosperous enterprises. At the onset of the war he had given the British government enough money to purchase a squadron of Spitfire aircraft. Immensely rich, he owned a number of properties including much of the land now occupied by Montreal's Dorval Airport, and, in the city, a palatial mansion where most of us were lodged. He also owned a lake in the Laurentian Mountains and a luxurious log-cabin house on its shore. Mr McConnell was quiet and polite; his wife, however, had a reputation as a difficult lady. My aunt was also strong-minded. I don't think there was ever a big row between them, rather an agreement reached after a few months that we should live separately. They were two ladies who liked to run things themselves. My aunt laid great stress on our independence and that was why she wanted the three of us to live in a separate establishment. This had repercussions for all of us because we had little money of our own with us, except for the few hundred pounds which my aunt had collected before we left and which was all we were legally allowed to take out. So we and the McConnell family parted company. The McConnells generously rented a little semi-detached house for us in the comfortable Westmount area of Montreal, and there we lived, Charles and I making the daily visit to school. We did not like the school (Selwyn House) or its headmaster much; small Canadian boys, for what reason I am still not sure, seemed much rougher than their American counterparts. The most we learnt was how to skate and play ice hockey, and not very well at that. The other occupant of our house was the maid, Elizabeth, a girl in her twenties, who is the only person I have ever met who came from Prince Edward Island, the smallest Canadian province, with a reputation for backwardness. Elizabeth certainly lived up to that. She had poor eyesight, was not very bright and wet her bed, although she was kind and gentle to us.

Our money dwindled, until eventually we were down to a very small sum saved by my aunt. She was a resourceful lady, sold some of the jewellery she had illegally brought with her and found English friends in Montreal, including some cousins, who lent her the odd sum. She also borrowed some money from Mrs Brocklebank, a remote cousin on my mother's side. One of her forebears, Spencer Madden, had been tutor to the unruly children of the Fourth Duke of Richmond when the family lived in Brussels. Mrs Brocklebank's book *Spencer at Waterloo* is an absorbing read, based on the unpublished manuscript letters between the young tutor and his father, a cleric at Lichfield Cathedral.

The letters are frank and funny. Mrs Brocklebank had three children with her in Canada about our age, who became great friends. She was a true bluestocking and a strict mother. She would not for instance allow her children to eat ice cream or drink Coca Cola. Despite this, we spent a happy summer holiday with them in Maine in 1942, in a place which had been a fashionable resort about 50 years before and had much faded charm.

My aunt gave us as much independence as she thought prudent. She sent us on shopping and other errands for her, which enabled us to learn a bit of French-Canadian in the process. I remember the tram conductor announcing one of the stops as 'Green Avenue/*Avenue Green*', presumably in case his French-Canadian passengers were confused by the English practice of placing the adjective before the noun. To cheer us all up, our aunt bought us a white kitten called Rodney, named after the battleship. Rodney looked sweet, but he was also a pest. He climbed a tall tree in our little garden and was too frightened to come down again on his own. The Montreal Fire Brigade had to rescue him. When we finally left Montreal, Rodney ran away and our efforts

9

to find him nearly made us miss our train. He was a wilful and obstinate cat. We eventually caught him and Aunt Molly took him to the RSPCA, who said they would find a new home for him. I was never quite sure whether she made this up to console us or not.

One day Charles and I left the house on our own and a large black dog ran out from our neighbour's house and bit my brother severely on the leg. What we didn't know was that, four generations earlier, our ancestor, the fourth Duke of Richmond, who had been Governor General of Canada and who was buried in Quebec Cathedral, had died from a bite of a dog or fox infected with rabies. We felt that something must in any case be done, and I rang the Montreal Police, quite bravely in retrospect, as I was only nine. A policeman called Les arrived in a car with a colleague, took my brother to hospital, had the wound cauterised and bandaged and then returned him home. My aunt was horrified when she came home and we told her the story, but I remember feeling smug. Les became quite a friend of ours, waving to us cheerily as he passed us on his rounds in his patrol car and enquiring after Charles's leg, which very soon healed up, although he still bears the scar.

We liked our little house in a modest but genteel suburb of Montreal. We spent our leisure time collecting stamps (Charles's hobby) and bubble gum, especially the brand that had a picture of a British warship on the packet. In winter, we spent the odd weekend skiing in the Laurentian Mountains, and, because the snow was often very deep, usually travelled by sleigh drawn by docile horses with sleigh bells. In the summer, we went fishing on the lakes, our catch being mainly inedible dogfish and the occasional trout. These we cooked on fires we lit near where our canoes were beached. It was an idyllic existence for a small boy.

2

Two Ghost Stories and a Grandfather

Goodwood ought to be the kind of house which has a spectacular ghost, but it does not appear to. There is something there, but it has proved elusive. There is a story about the third Duke's charger in the Peninsular War (named Busaco after the victory over the French in Portugal), which is reputed to be buried near or beneath the ice house which was built in Goodwood Park in the eighteenth century. On one occasion it frightened some tourist, who thought that they were being throttled when they were near where the horse is said to be buried, but my brother could never find the horse's remains.

A better story comes from Maisie, a spirited Scottish maid who worked at Goodwood when I was only a small boy, where her job was to clean some of the downstairs rooms including the small library, which my father and his predecessors used as an office. It is a charming room with a cantilevered gallery running round the wall which is full of bookcases and a little spiral staircase giving access to it. Some of the oldest books in the house are on its shelves, including the fourth Duchess of Richmond's old notebook written in her own hand, listing the people she had invited to her famous ball on the eve of the Battle of Waterloo.

One morning, very early, Maisie was dusting the gallery lined by bookcases when she looked down into the main room and at my father's desk beneath. She saw a shadowy figure seated in my father's chair. Its features were difficult to make out, but to Maisie, a down-to-earth Scot, there was no doubt she had seen a ghost. Terrified, she rushed to the housekeeper, Mrs Cowie, and the butler, Mr Marshall, who both persuaded her to calm down. There is just a hint in Maisie's account, which she sent to me some years later, that Mrs Cowie and Mr Marshall had earlier seen something similar themselves in the same room.

Maisie noted that the time and day of the apparition coincided exactly with the moment when my father had an accident in his car, from which he emerged unhurt, but Maisie drew no conclusion from this. She is now in an old people's home in Scotland and wrote to me about this. She also, incidentally, had something to say about the non-spectral inhabitants of the house. My mother, a few months earlier, had advertised for a cook in the *Morning Post*. She received replies from several candidates and decided to take the one she considered the best, a Miss Jane Stacey. Miss (thereafter called 'Mrs' in the way that senior servants were in those times) Stacey was the daughter of a Thames bargee who wore a flat cap and crossed scarves. Maisie, who did not much like Mrs Stacey's commanding role in the kitchen, predicted that before too long our family would be employing the entire Stacey family. She was right. Within a month or so my mother also employed three more Stacey sisters – Louise; Dorothy, the parlour maid (she had worked before coming to us for Winston Churchill's family); Marjorie, the head parlour maid, who held herself responsible for her sisters – and occasionally their mother too. There was a brother who for some reason we never employed, and the father stuck to his barge throughout. Mrs (Jane) Stacey stayed with us until she died, working for us regularly when needed. She married towards the end of the war, an RAMC sergeant (having had an earlier flirtation with another sergeant whom she referred to as her 'passing wartime fancy'). The husband she married in the end was an annoying person with no apparent intelligence or talent. But since his presence was essential to the domestic solidarity of the Stacey family, we thought he should be employed and my father had him taught bookbinding, which was only a moderate success but at least kept him most of the time busy below stairs.

Mrs Stacey was vigorous in her defence of all of us and our interests, and of course a stout defender also of the interests of her own family. She lived in the housekeeper's room in Goodwood for the last years of her life accompanied by dogs which smelt and yapped, and it was quite an ordeal to penetrate her room. But she was worth her weight in gold. She knew where everything was, and she was ferociously loyal, above all to my mother, to whom she was a great support.

The second ghost story came from Wendover, where my maternal grandfather (whom to my regret I never met) was for his closing years the rector until his death in the late 1920s. He and his wife and family lived in the large late-Victorian vicarage – now converted to an old people's home – near the church. Of his nine children, two boys (Arthur and Tommy) had been killed in World War I, both young officers in the Royal Berkshire Regiment. At the time of this story (the early 1920s), the youngest sons would have been sometimes at Wendover during the holidays from school and university. The second and third daughters – Molly and Elizabeth (Betty), my mother – were both in their twenties and lived in Wendover with their parents more or less permanently during this decade.

Molly and Betty shared a bedroom. One night Molly woke up to find a little girl, perhaps about twelve years old, standing at the foot of her bed. She had golden curls and wore a blue-and-white striped dressing gown. She put her head on one side and, apparently addressing Molly,

13

made a face and said, 'This is the face the boys make when mother kisses them before they go to school.' She then vanished. Molly, very frightened, shot across the room and joined Betty, who was still asleep in her bed. She woke her up and told her what had happened. She and Betty resolved to tell no one – partly because they did not want to spread unnecessary alarm in the household. But a few days later, at breakfast, their father said, 'An extraordinary thing happened to me last night. A little girl came into my room and stood over my bed. She had golden curls and wore a blue-and-white striped dressing gown.' Molly and Betty then told him their own story, and their father said he would do some research. He in due course discovered that a previous occupant of the vicarage had a little daughter who had died there of scarlet fever some years before and answered the description given by him and by Molly and Betty. He was sent a photograph of her, which unfortunately does not survive, but it was apparent that it was the same little girl who had appeared to him and Molly.

The little girl was seen once more by Molly. She ran through her bedroom one night waving a branch of some kind before disappearing. She did not speak on this occasion. Questioned on how she had seen the girl in the dark, Molly said she was surrounded by a light which enabled one to see her features quite clearly.

Molly (and from all accounts her father, and from my own observation) was a matter-of-fact person with both feet on the ground, and she took an undramatic view of apparitions. Although she saw no more ghosts in the vicarage she said that from time to time she heard children crying on the top floor and heard horses in the stables near by when they were empty. Much later on, after the war, Molly lived in a small flat on the top floor of 39 Hill Street, in Mayfair. This looked over a block of flats which had been burned and bombed in the war. It was a shell, with no staircase or floor, and Molly was surprised one day to see a girl standing on the top floor looking out of the window. She assumed this to have been a ghost, and she knew that a young girl had been killed there during the Blitz. Molly was neither frightened nor particularly surprised.

My grandfather was a good and conscientious rector, much liked by his flock, but his true interest lay in farming; hence his close friendship with his neighbour, Farmer Brown at Great Shefford whom, for reasons now forgotten, he christened James the son of Alphaeus. My grandfather was as much the squire as the rector and knew his parishioners very well. He once told the local rate collector, who was pestering him for an overdue payment, that he was the sort of person who indulged in secret sin (he knew a thing or two about the rate collector's clandestine love life). The rate collector did not call again.

He liked to listen occasionally at the door of the Methodist chapel in Great Shefford, and once to his delight heard the Minister saying to a member of his congregation, ''Ere, you be quiet, or I'll stuff the Bible down your throat.' And during World War I he would embarrass his children by asking any able-bodied young man he encountered not in uniform why he was not shouldering a musket. One day in the dining room, a stray cat jumped through an open window and made for my grandfather and perched on his head. Grandfather was unmoved. 'Seek ye the priesthood also,' he said.

Although physically strong, with his large family and many responsibilities, he was (it appears) not always as robust as he seemed. Every now and then he fell victim to what he called a 'sinking feeling'. When this happened he would go to the sideboard in the dining room where there were three bottles and take a large swallow from one of them, which evidently made him feel better. One day, with the symptoms of a sinking feeling starting to show themselves,

15

he went to the sideboard and took his usual swallow from the bottle. He immediately realised that something was wrong; namely the 'sinking feeling' mixture had been put in a different bottle and he had swallowed a lot of cleaning fluid which had replaced it. He ran next door where most of his family were assembled and told them what had happened. According to his account, no one took him seriously, and his plight evoked laughter rather than sympathy. Seeing that his family were no help, he rushed to his next-door neighbour, where James the son of Alphaeus lived. The latter had a friend staying with him, and my grandfather told him what had happened. There was a bit of a pause while this sank in, and then James's friend said, 'I wouldn't be lighting my pipe for a while if I was you, Rector.'

Grandfather died of a massive stroke in 1929, having a few days earlier walked a huge distance with his young grandson Tommy, in clerical garb, inspecting his rural deanery.

3

Goodwood Races

The main fame of Goodwood, then and now, rests on its horse racing. The racecourse, which was the family business also then and now, started informally in 1802. At the beginning, races were run between horses mainly owned by the officers of the Sussex militia on the crest of the South Downs called the Harroways. This is a flat but narrow ridge of land about two miles north of Goodwood House, running from east to west and ending with a run up the steep Trundle Hill, a Bronze Age camp, which acted as a brake for the finishers. The great horse St Simon, winner of the three-mile Goodwood Cup many years ago, enjoyed himself so much after winning his race he continued to gallop up the hill and down the other side before someone pulled him up.

Gradually, over the years, the crowds grew and paid a small sum for entry. Trundle Hill was the scene of many plebeian picnics, with whelks and jellied eels and of course much beer consumed by coach-loads of sportsmen from the East End of London and some from as far afield as Newcastle, year after year. The view of the actual racing from the hill was poor, but the parties on the hill were jolly and there were plenty of bookies present. There were only four days of racing a year, which yielded enough income to make it a profit-making enterprise, and this it has largely remained to this day. In the years that followed the world wars, when amusements for the public were few and scattered, the races – held on four days at the end of July (for the gentry this marked the end of the 'season') – drew immense crowds, perhaps three times the size seen now. Today they are much smaller, but there are now 21 days' racing (in the afternoon or evening) in the year, and many more local diversions.

For years the races were a royal occasion, with the monarch of the time present, usually with some race horses and often with a royal mistress who knew all sorts about horses (Lillie Langtry, too, was a frequent visitor though she never stayed at Goodwood House). The present Queen attended every other year, staying at Goodwood all four days, until 1970, when her children's school exams and holidays clashed with our dates and she could no longer join us.

My mother organised the social and all other aspects of the whole Race Week beautifully – not a bad effort for a country vicar's sixth child, which she was. The house nearly burst at its seams. Extra servants were drafted in: the nineteen-bedded room on the top floor of the house was filled with the guests' servants, who incidentally used to include the Duke of Portland's barber when he was staying in the house. My parents usually invited two friends each for Charles and me, a few of their own, and half a dozen or so of the Queen's own close friends, mostly horse-racing enthusiasts, which I think made a great difference to her enjoyment of her few days off, as she found the house full of the people she knew and liked most. She usually read or worked in her room in the morning, until about 12.30 when we all went up the wooded hills to the racecourse for lunch. This was always delicious, and my mother was a merry and relaxed hostess. After the races, it was back home for tea and dinner, the men wearing dinner jackets, not white ties. The ladies, in the hot July weather, wore long dresses with low or bare backs; and after dinner if it was warm we would sit on cushions on the steps outside the library, drinking

18

coffee and chatting. One particularly warm evening my father absent-mindedly stroked the bare back of the lady seated on the cushion in front of him. This was pleasant for my father and also for the lady. The only problem was that the lady's back was not my mother's, as he had thought, but the Queen's. My father desisted, and years later I asked the Queen if she remembered my father gently tickling her back one evening at Goodwood. The Queen said, no, she didn't remember that particular incident, but she had no doubt it took place. My father remembers her saying at the time, 'Do go on, Freddie.' I don't think he did.

We were all, of course, on our best behaviour, even when this involved an extremely tiring session in the early morning in the cricket nets, bowling at Prince Philip, who had a local charity cricket game to play a day or two later. Charles and I were exhausted by the bowling – I don't think we even got to bat, only Prince Philip. He could be a demanding guest.

My mother took particular charge of the welfare of visiting royal servants and once got a crossed line on her telephone which enabled her to listen to a visiting footman from Buckingham Palace talking to one of his female colleagues in London. The former spoke in glowing terms of Goodwood, the comfortable bedrooms, the food, the weather, and urged his friend to join him there. This offer was declined, perhaps out of a sense of propriety, but my mother was delighted, regarding it little short of a royal accolade.

After the royal party had left the races at Goodwood they went on for an hour or so to watch the polo at Cowdray. Every other year they stayed at Arundel Castle, about ten miles away, with the Duke and Duchess of Norfolk, which my family always felt must have been an elderly and stuffy party compared to ours.

With the races over, we took off for a holiday of our own in Cornwall, to a bungalow designed by my father at

Constantine Bay, near Padstow, on the rocky north coast of Cornwall. We all shrimped and swam, and my brother and I shot rabbits in the next-door field with Stanley Old, who ran the post office and local general store, and was the village's fount of knowledge and general philosopher. My father planted a little garden, for which he employed a part-time Cornish gardener called Ephraim, who had watched the Coronation on television and asked my father about 'the tea cosy Your Highness [sic] had to wear on your head all day'. My mother meanwhile indulged in what she said was her favourite hobby – sitting in a deckchair, with a 1920s-style ladies' tennis shade on her head, reading the latest *Tatler*. It was as unlike the grandeur of Goodwood Race Week as you could possibly get. Some time much later, my father sold the house to (I think) the Wolfsons, and Mrs Thatcher was their guest there several times on short holidays – not perhaps ideal for her, as none of us could envisage her shrimping, surfing, shooting rabbits or even paddling.

I think Charles and I started going to Goodwood Race Week around 1937 when I was about six. It was exciting, and its rural setting as beautiful as it is today. One day, some magnate of the turf offered to introduce me to Gordon Richards, many times Champion Jockey, and wearing his silks before the next race. I asked him if he was going to win this. Gordon Richards replied enigmatically, 'I'd have a little something on me if I were you.' This seemed to me – small as I was – as good a tip as I could get anywhere and I persuaded someone to put a small bet on for me. The race was run and Gordon Richards' horse came in third. This was a salutary lesson. It didn't stop me betting later on from time to time, but it made me prudent, a small-stakes person, and I usually have my encounter with Gordon Richards in the back of my mind when approaching the bookies, however excellent the write-up from tipsters, the form books, or the many friends who believe themselves to be in the know.

The war brought all this to an end, and there were no more races until it ended. Life for us all changed.

4

The 'Tiddly Quid'

There then occurred another of those things which from time to time deflect the direction of your life. We had an uncle, Noel, one of my mother's brothers, who was a bishop in the Church of England, and also a DSO and an MC from World War I. He was Bishop of Newcastle, which he liked, until 1958, and thereafter Bishop of Ely, which he didn't – he would have much preferred a rougher, more urban diocese. He told a fellow American bishop, named Thomas Matthews, about our predicament in Canada, who immediately said, 'Send them down here [he lived in Princeton, New Jersey] and we will look after them for the duration of the war.' So, a few weeks later we found ourselves on the night train from Montreal via New York to Trenton to be met by the bishop in an imposing black car driven by his amiable chauffeur, Walter Roteman. Walter was very much a member of the family with a wife, Dolly, who was the cook – and a very good one, too. Walter had very short legs, and the bishop used to say that he didn't really walk, he sort of twinkled.

I remembered the bishop well that day in a dark clerical suit with a straw hat on his head with a Princeton University ribbon of orange and black round it. He had for some years been the Bishop of New Jersey and before that Professor of Dogmatic Theology at Columbia University in New York. In retirement, he now lived in a large Edwardian mansion in Princeton, his old college town. He was very rich, at least by American clerical standards. His wife, who must have been in her sixties, was a Proctor and Gamble heiress, gentle and beautiful, who invariably wore long silk dresses and a lace cap. I asked her one day about the lace cap, which looked very well on her, and she said that she had decided it was proper to wear one when she became a grandmother. I never saw her without it.

The bishop had several children. Tom, the eldest and only son, was then editor of *Time* magazine and the right-hand man of Henry Luce, the press magnate and publisher. Tom was an intellectual as well as a journalist who wrote a number of attractive books and memoirs. His pretty wife, Julie, died young, leaving him four sons. The second of these, John, was nearest to us in age and our particular friend, who later had a successful career with Radio Free Europe. He was an exceptionally civilised boy, very kind to the two small English visitors who had attached themselves to his family, and one of the nicest people I have ever met. His father, Tom, was later married two more times, once to Martha Gelhorn, the adventurous ex-wife of Ernest Hemingway, and a ground-breaking journalist and author of travel and other books which are still widely read and greatly admired.

Every morning about eight o'clock my brother and I would get on our bicycles, ancient second-hand machines purchased by my aunt, and ride the two or more miles to school through the African-American quarter of the little town and then past the grand clubs to which many of the better-heeled undergraduates at Princeton University belonged. Meanwhile, the bishop assembled family prayers in the chapel he had built adjoining his house. Everyone was there, from guests staying in the house to the servants, of which there must have been half a dozen. The service was rather like a shortened form of matins, prayers predominating.

23

I do not remember any hymn singing, but there was a moment when the bishop prayed at length for friends and acquaintances of his, many of whom he must have met in earlier travels around the world. My aunt regularly attended this service. Soon she noticed that the list of those for whom the bishop prayed changed from time to time. Some were invariably included, such as the Little Sisters of Wu-Hu, who we thought must have been Chinese nuns in the Anglican Church whom the bishop had encountered at some stage in China. Some names were also dropped permanently, not to reappear. We concluded that these were acquaintances who had fallen out with the bishop or who had caused offence in some other unspecified way. Prayers lasted for about 20 minutes, by which time Charles and I had arrived at school.

At school, Charles and I were at least a year or two younger than our class contemporaries. We were small and thin with squeaky voices. Our contemporaries seemed to be twice our size. They shaved and had deep voices and girlfriends. My brother and I got treated rather like class mascots and made many friends, who sometimes threw us from one to the other as in American football. At the year's end, the school magazine published a 'will' in which the leaving senior boys all bequeathed something to their juniors. I remember my bequest was from a boy called Morehouse, a huge young man with a growing beard, kindly and gentle. His bequest to me was his 'streamlined' figure. He was anything but streamlined, but chose so to describe himself in his class 'will'. A gentle giant.

Meanwhile, there was another family member in the house, Aunt Jane, the bishop's sister. She had spent most of her life in France but never seemed to have managed the language. She infuriated the bishop, I recall, by giving the word 'angelus' its French pronunciation. She was lame and rather deaf and had a problem with wind. Whenever she walked she attempted to disguise her windy noises with the

24

tap of her walking stick on the floor. No one was deceived, least of all my brother and myself who were waiting for these moments every time poor Aunt Jane walked through the house. She had once been married but had no children. She claimed to have a distinguished English lover who sent her flowers every day, but he clearly existed only in her imagination. Her nephew wrote a touching but critical little piece about her and after that no one heard anything more about the lover. She was a sad but not easy character, and she must have irritated the bishop greatly. She appeared happy and comfortable at Merwick, the bishop's house.

The bishop had other children – all daughters – the youngest of whom, Harriet, had died of blood poisoning at an early age. Her room had been on the top floor, now occupied by us; and my aunt and my brother, both with a taste for the occult, were sure that her presence was still there. There were noises in the night, mysteriously from a typewriter, long after any typing by other people in the house had ceased. We rather wished we had met Harriet, who was by all accounts pretty and charming. The room still had her clothes in it. My aunt and brother and I sometimes played planchette in the evenings in the vain hope that we might make contact with Harriet, or anyone else for that matter. We never did.

On summer nights, going to bed when it was still daylight, we were entertained by Princeton undergraduates singing college songs on the steps of Nassau Hall, the oldest building in the university and its centre of activity. These were mostly rugged football songs encouraging the Princeton football team which had a good but tough record. The songs were mostly hearty and clean, although I do remember one chant ridiculing the supposed effeminacy of their Harvard Ivy League rivals. The chant went: 'H, A, R, V, A, R, D, HARVARD, HARVARD, WHEEEE!' It was all very respectable. Most people seemed sober, but it was frustrating

25

listening to this jolly gathering in broad daylight. It would have been more fun to have been on the steps of the hall too, and singing along. But we were both too small.

We played the normal American sports, especially baseball, which left my brother and myself with a liking for that superb and exciting game that has always remained with us. We would watch a lot of college football and baseball and, Princeton being too small for its own professional team, we became enthusiastic fans of the Brooklyn Dodgers who had a nationwide appeal comparable to teams like Manchester United or Real Madrid today. They were a picturesque bunch springing from different nationalities. Their hero was their coach, Leo Durocher, otherwise known as 'Leo the Lip', whose English was barely intelligible but who drove his popular team with great success. They and the New York Yankees usually shared the championship between them. The Yankees' great star was, of course, Joe DiMaggio, who later married Marilyn Monroe. The Yankees had an equally picturesque coach called Casey Stengal, also largely incoherent, who talked a language of his own widely known as Stengalese. It was he who once said of the Giants, another rival New York team: 'See those guys over there? They are the Giants. They are nice guys. Nice guys don't win games.'

The Princeton Country Day (PCD) school was a cheerful place. We were very well taught in a happy atmosphere. I returned there once 15 years later when it had been amalgamated with one of the best girl schools in the area and its standards were very high indeed.

In 1943, after nearly two years at the PCD, it was decided to send my brother and myself home to England. The reason was that we were approaching the age for entry into the English public school system. It seemed not to have occurred to my parents that 1943 was about the time when U-boat activity was at its highest and we were exposed to far greater risks than we would have been had we remained at home in 1940. My father and mother were by coincidence themselves in Washington at the time. An RAF technical expert, my father was on a mission to the USA to seek components used in British aircraft, and he made the highly irregular arrangements with naval friends for our return home. I was then eleven, and my brother, Charles, one year older. We were taken back to England on an ancient battleship, with about two dozen other small boys for all of whom this was a great adventure. My brother and I travelled down from Washington to Norfolk, Virginia, the big US naval base, to catch our ship, spending two nights on board an aircraft carrier called the *Indomitable* before embarking on the battleship HMS *Royal Sovereign* – nicknamed the 'Tiddly Quid' by its crew – which took us eventually via the Clyde to Gourock.

It was nearly a three-week journey across the Atlantic. The whole scheme was a highly unofficial one to say the least. It had been arranged on the old boy network, and the regulations would certainly not allow it today. We were on board because the naval attaché knew the captain of the *Royal Sovereign* and had arranged for us to travel on it unofficially. The British Ambassador's wife wanted apparently to travel on it too, but the *Royal Sovereign*'s captain was adamant. Schoolboys were one thing, but ambassadors' wives another. Among other things she would have to pass through the marines' quarters while on board, and that was totally unacceptable.

Our memories of the return trip on the *Royal Sovereign* are not happy ones. I had rather wanted to enter the navy previously, liking their smart blue uniform, and the likelihood of a life of travel and adventure, but I soon dropped that plan. Most of us small boys slept in hammocks, or on camp beds, in what had been the captain's dining room in peacetime. The cold was intense (it was now October), and my brother and I used to take off our shoes and socks and rub our feet on the leather upholstered chairs to warm them up. There was one bucket in the corner of the room which you could be sick into. The ship was immensely slow – I think its speed averaged not more than about 11 knots, and a fire in one of its boilers slowed it down further. We were escorted across the Atlantic by four frigates. In addition to being old and slow the *Royal Sovereign* was seriously undermanned. It had some new Oerlikon anti-aircraft batteries but few people to operate them, and I remember seeing a young rating having a terrible time learning his basic training at the hands of a not very tolerant gunnery expert. There were occasional alerts about the presence of U-boats in the vicinity, and we saw our destroyer escorts dropping depth charges in the hope of blowing them up. To our disappointment, there was no result, although reports indicate that there may have been a U-boat in the area. Either the depth charges missed the U-boats or there weren't any there in the first place. We shall never know.

The chaplain, whom we all heartily disliked, was technically in charge of the group of boys. He had a red nose with a drip on the end of it, and no sense of humour. My brother discovered he was also the group's censor (all letters to and from us were censored), and thereafter many of our letters home included offensive drawings of him. The person who really kept an eye on us was a sympathetic and tough marine sergeant called Gilbert. He was cheerful and kindly, knew us all by name, and seemed to like us. He told me that what he really looked forward to in England was a pint of warm beer. On the way home we stopped for two days at the Allied naval base at Argentia Bay in Newfoundland; the first time I had visited that bleak island – and probably the last. It had a primitive NAAFI, where you could get things like Hershey bars, the American mass-selling chocolate bars. After what seemed an age but was only about ten freezing days, we sailed up the Clyde, passed Dunoon and docked at Gourock, from there taking the night train through mist and rain via Greenock to London. I am indebted for this short account to an old friend of mine called Maldwin Drummond who was on the same ship with his brother. They had been at school elsewhere in the United States. Maldwin, a boy of intelligence and charm, who subsequently did his reserve military service with me in the Green Jackets, is now a person of distinction in Hampshire and yachting circles, living on his estate on the Solent. He has written an eloquent and well-researched account of our trip which has been published.

The train at Greenock, bound for London, was cold and full of soldiers and cigarette smoke. You could not see out of the windows because they had some kind of mesh on them to lessen the effect of bomb blasts. Even if you had been able to see through the window you would have been none the wiser, as all the station, street and road signs had been removed to confuse a possible invader. Eventually, we arrived at King's Cross Station, and were met later at the Dorchester Hotel, for some reason, by another aunt, Doris Vyner, one of my father's two sisters. She put us up in London for a couple of nights before we went home to Goodwood.

Goodwood had at that time not yet become a hospital but a Royal Army Medical Corps depot and transit camp. All the furnishings and decorations in the house had been removed, leaving the family with three or four rooms – the kitchen, my father's study, and bedrooms for my parents, my brother and myself. There not being enough lavatories in the house, three little red brick outhouses had been added to what in happier days had been the library, the main hall and the yellow drawing room. Linoleum covered the floors. The books in the large and small libraries were boarded up in their bookshelves. The sound of army boots echoed everywhere.

Meanwhile my Aunt Doris felt it was essential to find us

a tutor, on the grounds that our American education must have placed us far behind our English contemporaries. It turned out that the standard of education we were given in America was just as good. To be sure, my Aunt Doris nevertheless hired a tutor, Mr Bransome. I think he had been a preparatory schoolmaster most of his life and had now retired to Tunbridge Wells. He wore a trim, old-fashioned brown tweed suit, and a brown bowler hat when he went out. His manners were Edwardian. He kissed my aunt's hand a lot and invariably addressed her as 'dear lady'. He drank a lot of tea, which Charles and I thought he viewed as a cure for the problem he had with constipation. He was helped in this by my mother, by now returned to Goodwood, when she found out that liquid paraffin purchased from the chemist and properly prepared, was just as good as normal salad oil, which was of course unobtainable in the war. Unfortunately, the Food Ministry found this out too and spoiled the salad oil by adding peppermint flavouring. Mr Bransome was a gentle but firm disciplinarian ('Don't play, boy, don't play,' he would say), but a superb tutor. He had my brother and me reading the essays of Charles Lamb, and he introduced us to Shakespeare and the English poets. He had a straggly grey moustache, a red nose and a fondness for port. When the time came, he triumphed. My brother passed into the top form at Eton, and I, nearly two years younger, into the appropriate one a year behind. I remember him not just with amusement, but with genuine affection. Mr Bransome tolerated the austerity of a huge stately home and military transit camp, staffed by only two servants – Mrs Stacey, the cook/housekeeper (Nanny had by then left us), and Miss Clarke, my mother's maid. But I think he was happy in the still relatively palatial surroundings. He was especially fond of our Aunt Doris.

It took us a little while to get used to England again. In some ways, nothing, it seemed, had changed since we were last there in the late 1930s, but it certainly differed from the United States. The sky seemed somehow greyer and closer to the ground. There were, of course, virtually no cars, whereas in America nearly everyone seemed to have one. Everything was rationed – including nearly all food, as well as sweets, clothing and alcoholic drinks. There was a wartime atmosphere, which was dreary compared to the cheerful colour and liveliness of the USA.

5

Eton

I was especially lucky at Eton where I started in Mr Kerry's House, this being one of the only two remaining vacant places in the school. You could always tell when Kerry had been in your room because there was a slight aroma of whisky. He was succeeded for my last two years by the gentle and tolerant Philip Snow, just demobilised from the Royal Navy. Although I had some good friends in the House, it had more than the average number of bullies, philistines and semi-literate thugs, most of whom would never have got into the school today. Many of them, in their old age, are now, of course, respected and responsible people in the tiny provincial rural worlds they probably inhabit.

I was equally lucky in my 'classical beak', or tutor, in overall charge of my studies. The first of these was Oliver Hunkin, a talented cartoonist, and son of the Bishop of Truro. I was put in the school sanatorium shortly after my arrival because I had an attack of the highly infectious pink-eye (conjunctivitis), and Oliver Hunkin kindly visited me regularly, reading aloud to me because reading was forbidden for pink-eye patients, especially the works of Stephen Leacock ('Guido the Gimlet of Ghant', 'Gertrude the Governess', etc.), but he often laughed so much that his spectacles misted up and he could not go on.

When I got too old for Oliver Hunkin, and became a history specialist at 16, my tutor was Giles St Aubyn, the youngest son of Lord St Levan of St Michael's Mount in Cornwall and Harold Nicolson's nephew. Giles had got a First in History at Oxford after leaving the navy and was only a few years older than me. He was an extremely able historian and biographer, and one of his aims was to get me a History scholarship at Oxford. This he did, by the simple expedient of predicting the sort of questions likely to be put to me. He also accused me, accurately, of idleness; and when I won the Rosebery history prize, consisting of books, he threw them at me one by one and said I didn't deserve them. He adopted the same attitude (also alleging luck) when two 'halves' (terms) later I won an open scholarship to Worcester College, Oxford. I am also deeply indebted to Giles for his refusal to show me the report which my first university examiner (Hugh Trevor Roper of Christ Church, later Lord Dacre) had written on me, on the grounds that it could only discourage me. My papers must have been awful.

I was a successful and happy Etonian, the usual mixture of innocence and arrogance, a little too proud of my academic prowess, such as it was, and as vain as any of my contemporaries.

My three best friends were witty young men of artistic talent – Bruce Whineray, Tony Dennis and John Bowles. Bruce Whineray died tragically of leukaemia at the age of 40, and Tony Dennis, a talented racing driver, was killed when his car went off the track at Goodwood, of all places, in one of the first serious motor races he took part in. John Bowles always said that he would end up in prison or in the church. He was a very close friend indeed, but dropped out of my life after leaving Eton, and was only discovered again years later by a fellow ex-schoolboy, as a missionary priest in the outback of Australia, married, with several children, devout and considerably less irreverent.

Two memorable events occurred when I was a little boy

at Eton. In the winter of 1946, the Thames, swollen by heavy rainfall, overflowed its banks and Eton was flooded. Most classes were cancelled and the boys moved about in little rowing boats. (Where did they come from?) Eventually, after a few days' idleness, the school sent us all home – two weeks early, rightly fearing the outbreak of disease when the water subsided. We were all happy about this, me notably because it meant no more mathematics classes with an ancient and bullying beak called Mr H.K. ('Bloody Bill') Marsden, who turned all his classes into 45 minutes of terror for his little pupils. He was the only housemaster at the time who personally beat his boys for transgressions, however minor, and would now, 50 years later, have been sacked in disgrace. I recall only one light moment. He said to Charlie Hambro, who was in his and my class, 'Hambro, I have only ever taught one boy more stupid than yourself and that was your father.' Hambro's father, Sir Olaf Hambro, was at the time deputy governor of the Bank of England.

The war ended when I was fourteen. VE Day was memorable. Anarchy prevailed. No beak was in sight. We started with a most satisfactory water fight with Mr Lambart's House next door. One of our boys got hold of a hosepipe and drenched any of Lambart's boys who tried to escape. I recollect that Lambart's boys extracted a terrible revenge. After a while the whole House, most of us dripping wet, marched as a single unit up the High Street to Windsor, where we milled about and made as much noise as possible. The Captain of Games, in later years an Olympic yachtsman, incessantly blew a trumpet which he had acquired somewhere. He would never have been a candidate for a symphony orchestra. Eventually, and miraculously, we returned to our House (the Manor House), still together in a semi-disciplined group. Mr Kerry, whose House it was, checked that we were all back (in retrospect I am sure some of us were not) and removed our gas masks which were hanging from our

34

bedroom doors. 'You won't be needing these now,' he observed. Nor, even better, would we ever have to sleep again in the squalid air-raid shelter.

Among the temporary beaks in my day at Eton was Kenneth Rose, the brilliant historian and royal biographer who taught me history and remains a close friend nearly sixty years later. Having served in the Welsh Guards during the war, he came to replace a senior history master who had suddenly retired through ill health. In the way that Etonians have, one boy put up his hand in class and said, 'May I ask you a question, sir? How much do they pay you here?' Kenneth rose to the occasion: 'My dear boy,' he said, 'what they pay me here wouldn't keep me in cigars for a month.' The Headmaster, Claude Aurelius Elliott, heard of the episode and was not pleased.

Before two compulsory years in the army (1949–1951), as I have said, I won an open History scholarship to Worcester College, Oxford, the oldest (in point of buildings) and one of the most beautiful in the university. Its provost was J.C. Masterman, a historian who had a certain aura of mystery about him, having been deputy head of MI5 in the war. His ambition, usually achieved, was to see his undergraduates into successful careers when they left. After the provost came the vice provost and dean, Colonel C.H. Wilkinson, who had served in the Guards in World War I, a brave and unusual soldier who was a leading authority on the Cavalier poets, a noted bibliophile, and for reasons never clearly explained to me, full-back for Blois football team during the period of his service in France. A large man with a deceptively intimidating manner, the dean instructed each year's intake of undergraduates on the college rules. One was about cars. 'You shall invariably,' he said, 'not keep a car in Oxford until at least your second year, when I shall decide whether or not to give you permission.' After my first year I duly wrote to him. 'My dear Dean,' I said, 'now that I have been at Oxford for one year, may I have your permission to keep a car there?' The car was an ancient Austin which my father and brother had owned for many years. The dean's answer was to the point. 'My dear Gordon Lennox,' it said, 'I have received your letter requesting that you keep a car at Oxford now that you are entering your second year. The art of life lies in the regulation of the mind and not in the whisking about of the body. You shall not, like Puck, put a girdle round Oxford in 40 minutes.' His letter went on in this vein for another four pages with Shakespearean quotations, but at no point did he say whether I had his permission or not. I therefore assumed I had it, and everyone seemed satisfied. One also had to ask the dean for special permission to stay out late. He said on one occasion that if I got back very late I should not wake the porter. This was an open invitation to climb into the college by means which were illegal and involved a furtive journey through the gardens of other colleges and private houses. I do not remember anyone ever getting caught or suffering the consequences.

I once asked the dean to Goodwood to look at the libraries there, with Lionel Robinson, who was one of his great friends, and an antiquarian bookseller of great knowledge and distinction (his shop was in Pall Mall). We let the two of them loose in the two mainly eighteenth-century libraries, and to our delight they each came up with the same short list of rarities. The dean also liked a wager. He once lunched with me at my digs (others there were four undergraduate friends, Kerry St Johnston, David Hennessy, John Robinson and Peregrine Pollen). The dean claimed that today's boys were not up to the standard of his own contemporaries athletically, among whom, he said, some could row, ride and run a mile within 15 consecutive minutes. We challenged this, and put forward Peregrine Pollen as our challenger. Peregrine, a natural athlete, trained with the help of a

36

university miler, a swift point-to-point horse, Garth Royal, and an experienced sculler, and completed the course on the Thames in under 15 minutes. The dean was delighted, and the trophy, a nineteenth-century gold sovereign, now sits on the table at dinners of the Worcester Kingsley Dining Club (named after the brother of the novelist Charles Kingsley) with a little explanation of its origin. The dean invited only one friend to the event, the writer and explorer Peter Fleming, who wrote the story up discreetly and elegantly for the *Spectator*.

The other dons at Worcester were a distinguished lot, including a great friend of mine called Professor Teddy Hall, who proved that the Piltdown Man was a fake, and devised the system of carbon dating by which it is possible to calculate with great accuracy the age of ancient and archaeological objects. He also threw parties which (to borrow a phrase from P.G. Wodehouse) 'staggered humanity'. He would ask congenial friends with many pretty girls, and the party would normally end up with complaints from the neighbours and sometimes from the police. He was a joy to be with. He was once caught out in some illegal escapade with his close friend and fellow undergraduate John Smith. The proctor (the university policeman) demanded their names. 'Teddy Hall,' said Teddy Hall (which was also the colloquial name for St Edward Hall, one of the colleges); 'John Smith,' said John Smith. This was quite enough for the proctor, who brought them before the appropriate disciplinary authority.

My own tutor at the time was a young don called Harry Pitt, a liberal and open-minded teacher with an inquiring mind, who was later himself the dean. Although an outstanding historian, to the regret of us all, he never wrote a book. One term, he had two pupils whom he taught together at a weekly tutorial. One was me, the other was a communist party member. His communism was not a youthful enthusiasm but something handed down from his parents who were both

37

Communist Party members themselves. Harry said he could do nothing to convert him from Marxism, but at least he could make him a good Marxist and he bent his efforts to that end.

When I left Oxford without much idea in my head of what to do next, it was the provost, J.C. Masterman, who steered me in the direction of the Foreign Office. A senior officer in MI5 in the war, he had a good idea of how government and Whitehall worked. He admitted Rupert Murdoch to the college, and two out of the three Sainsbury brothers, and clearly saw who would be useful benefactors to the college in the future. He got this right. I somehow survived the long drawn-out Foreign Office examination process (John Sparrow, then the Warden of All Souls, presided over the examiners) and that settled my life for the next 34 years.

My next-door neighbour at Worcester in my second year was an Ampleforth boy called Sandy Llewellyn. Unlike most of us, he had seen active service when doing his stint in the army with the Cameronians, fighting the Communist guerrillas in Malaya. He insisted at an early stage of our relationship that I accompany him to a course of lectures on Bishop Grosesteste of Lincoln (1175–1253), given by a distinguished don from central Europe called Dr Callus. I objected at first because my interest in the bishop was minimal. But I soon found out Sandy's real interest lay in the doctor's vague grasp of dates (he confused centuries not just years) and the certainty that, carried away by his subject, he would miss his footing on the podium and fall flat on his face. He didn't let us down.

The scholars' duties were light: once a week in term to read the lesson in morning chapel, and once a week to say grace before dinner in hall. The grace was the longest I have ever heard. The scholar appointed banged the table very loudly with a gavel. He then read grace at top speed, and there was scattered applause if he had been judged to break the speed record. The grace went like this:

Nos miseri homines et egeni, pro cibis quos nobis ad corporis subsidium benigne es largitus, tibi Deus omnipotens, Pater caelestis, gratias reverenter agimus; simul obsecrantes, ut iis sobrie, modeste, atque grate utamur. Insuper petimus, ut cibum angelorum, verum panum caelestem, verbum Dei aeternum. Dominum nostrum Jesum Christum, nobis impertiaris: utque illo mens nostra pascatur, et per carnum et sanguinem ejus foveamur, alamur, et corroboremur.

The translation of this is:

We unhappy and unworthy men do give thee most reverent thanks, Almighty God, our heavenly Father, for the victuals which thou hast bestowed on us for the sustenance of the body, at the same time beseeching thee that we may use them soberly, modestly and gratefully. And above all we beseech thee to impart to us the food of angels, the true bread of heaven, the eternal word of God, Jesus Christ our Lord, so that the mind of each of us may feed on him and that through his flesh and blood we may be sustained, nourished and strengthened.

Sandy, who was also like me a scholar, was very clever but very idle. He drank as much whisky as he could lay his hands on, and later on used to stay with us for a while when we were posted overseas by the Foreign Office. He turned up at the Madrid Embassy when we were there one August, and the temperature was hovering about 100 degrees, and announced that he had brought the good weather with him.

The dean wanted a picture (or rather a conversation piece) of some of his undergraduates and commissioned Edward Halliday, a distinguished portrait painter and Royal Academician, to paint a group of six or seven of us in my room in the late eighteenth-century quad. We were all public schoolboys, and I think some of our fellow undergraduates felt the dean had been too selective in his choice. Edward Halliday's works are to be found in many museums and private homes. He was cheerful and talkative and his car was full of paintings and accessories. Among the latter was always a bottle of gin. Petrol was in very short supply, and one of us expressed surprise that a car which had run out of petrol could run on gin. Halliday explained that this was not the purpose. If his car ran out of petrol, he drank the gin. He subsequently painted a head-and-shoulders portrait of my father and a companion portrait of my mother, which made her look fierce and not the lovely and funny person she always was.

My first room at Worcester was in the eighteenth-century block immediately opposite that of my brother's future brother-in-law, Wilfrid Grenville Grey, a clever but eccentric person who was reading theology on a scholarship with the vague idea of entering the church. This was enough for the various undergraduate Christian groups, who tried to get him to join them. His room tended to be full of Anglican, Catholic and, above all, Evangelical groups seeking to 'get him'. He resisted them all. His later career involved running an ecumenical college in Zambia, working for the notoriously difficult Canon Collins of St Paul's, marrying a well-born Zulu lady by whom he had three children, briefly becoming one of the Archbishop of Canterbury's private secretaries, and finally writing a book on the United Nations designed for those not interested in its purpose or its working. His great strength, or weakness, concerned cricket. He was convinced that if he could develop the perfect googly he would have discovered the secret of life. Unfortunately his googlies rarely succeeded in their objective, apart from one occasion when, to the latter's annoyance, he bowled out the captain of the Winchester XI ('Buster' Gard) first ball with a googly that bounced at least three times on the way to the wicket.

All political parties, too, appeared to have a recruiting officer with the aim of getting new blood into their organisations. One of the first such we received was Rupert Murdoch, who at the time represented the Oxford University Socialist Club, which I seem to recall was to the left of the Labour Club. I decided in the end not to join anything which had either secular or religious motives in mind. Rupert, an Australian devoted then and now to his college, was a cheerful young extrovert who moved from left to right across the political spectrum until he was more or less where he is now. I once went on a reading party with him in our last year and found him an agreeable companion. Even at that time he was clearly driven by the ambition to surpass his father as the biggest press magnate in Australia.

6

Army

Like most of my contemporaries, I did my two-year
compulsory military service, followed by three in the Territorial
Reserve, and I don't think my experience differed much
from theirs. On my first night in the army at Bushfield
Camp (just outside Winchester), where the Green Jackets
were trained, a cockney boy in the next-door bed said,
'Excuse me, are you Lord Gordon Lennox?' I said, 'Yes.'
And he said, 'Well, I am Lord Waghorn.' And we proceeded
on that basis as long as we were in the same hut. After
some weeks tough initial training I joined a potential Officers'
Squad, with a number of friends including Nicholas Eden
(Anthony Eden's son and my close friend and neighbour at
Goodwood) and John Eccles, the ex-head boy at Winchester
whose best man I would be a few years later. A few weeks
later we were joined by Peregrine Pollen, of whom more
below. The three of us had previously spent a summer
vacation in the USA in a car lent to us by one of Peregrine's
friends, driving from New York to Victoria, British Columbia,
down the West Coast to Los Angeles and thence back to
New York. We had the odd row, but parted good friends.
Sometimes we stayed (self-invited) with rich family friends,
otherwise in miserable discomfort in our borrowed Chevrolet.
My chief memories are the niceness of the Americans, the
beauty of Arizona and New Mexico, and some amiable girls
in Pittsburgh and Los Angeles.

We and the other riflemen in my intake who had passed the entry examination for Officer Cadet School were left at the Winchester Regimental Depot for some weeks with nothing much to do until the platoon immediately above us left Eaton Hall Officer Cadet School, graduated and made room for a new lot. The huge, forbidding Eaton Hall – formerly the home of the Dukes of Westminster – housed about one-third of the cadets. The remainder, including me, were in huts, which were in fact more comfortable. I was in one with several others – John Eccles being the senior under officer with three or four others, like me, junior under officers. Every week, my mother sent me a delicious game pie from Fortnum and Mason, which we shared for breakfast, giving us another welcome quarter of an hour in bed. We survived the rigours of battle camp in Cornwall, where we fired live ammunition and performed gruelling feats such as route marches, which demonstrated how fit we had become. We also survived many tongue lashings from senior non-commissioned officers who, I think, found Green Jacket drill sloppy and insufficiently precise (they were probably right). 'Slam your Jesus butt, sir!' shouted Sergeant Major Evans when we were ordered to slope arms. This was the first time, incidentally, that I had ever heard the word 'Jesus' used as an adjective.

John Eccles and I formed a light machine-gun team in the final exercise at camp and nearly had a fatal accident. A bullet got stuck in the barrel of our gun. The next bullet did not quite fit into the barrel behind the first. If it had, John and I could both have been nastily wounded by the resulting explosion of the barrel. Fortunately this did not happen, and our lives followed the normal round until the course ended. Then there was the usual passing-out parade, preceded by a service in the large Victorian chapel of the big house. Sergeant Pile of the Grenadier Guards had detailed our duties for the big day. 'You look a holy sort of

bugger,' he said to me cheerfully, 'you can read the f******
lesson.'

Socially, the atmosphere was curious. We were often
treated by the NCOs, all regular soldiers with wartime
experience, with disdain and contempt but not unmixed with
a certain affection. Thus, they called us 'Sir' but in all other
respects ignored the fact that within weeks we were all
likely to be officers and would order them about in totally
different circumstances.

My fellow riflemen at Winchester and Eaton Hall were a
mixed and amusing lot. My own platoon had a sergeant
called Hurlock, a huge craggy man with a nice sense of
humour. We also had in our number, and I suppose there
were about 20 of us, a riflemen recruit who had come into
the army on the same day as me, an East End Londoner
called Simpson. Simpson was not an elegant person and
had trouble with his drill movements. One of the most
intricate of these was the 'present arms' employed on highly
formal occasions and always if there were any member of
the Royal Family at the parade. On receiving the order,
Simpson clutched his rifle in the 'present arms' position
and somehow managed to look not as if he was carrying
out a mark of respect for the visiting royal person but as if
he was crouching behind his rifle for some unseemly and
improper purpose. On one parade, I remember Sergeant
Hurlock creeping up behind him and yelling in his ear so
that all the rest of us on the parade ground could hear, the
words 'Simpson, are you in ecstasy?'

I was also assigned guard duty from time to time, which
meant joining a small group of riflemen who stationed
themselves overnight in the guard room as, I suppose, a
kind of permanent sentry detachment. My little group was
in charge of a corporal called Tofts, the sanitary corporal,
whose job was essentially non-belligerent and involved
cleaning out and inspecting the washrooms and lavatories

in the camp. Tofts had strong political views, or rather prejudices. He also asked me if I was Lord Gordon Lennox and again I admitted that I was. 'Ha!', said Corporal Tofts, 'I thought I smelt a f****** aristocrat in here.'

One of the oddities of my National Service was that my brother, also a National Service man, was second in command of 'B' Company, the Green Jackets holding company at Winchester for riflemen who, having completed their basic training, were held at the depot for sometimes up to three months while their future postings were decided. Among them were a lot of 18- and 19-year-olds destined to become officers. These aspirants for commissions were placed in what amounted to a queue while they waited an unspecified time before there was a vacancy at Eaton Hall. My brother, who never lacked imagination, devised a plan for dealing with these young and underemployed riflemen – vaguely billed as an 'initiative scheme'. He divided the 18 or so young riflemen into teams of two, and assigned each team various tasks to complete, some of a very non-military nature. The team which completed its tasks first was the winner.

I teamed up with Rifleman Michael Pimbury, who had been at school at Cheltenham, an agreeable and cultivated person who later became president of the Oxford University Dramatic Society (OUDS). Michael and I were allotted a number of tasks. One was to obtain a wasps' nest, another was to ask the owner of St Michael's Mount in Cornwall how he reached his island home in the winter when there was a high tide and no causeway. Another was to obtain a bottle of vodka (signed) from the Russian Embassy in London; another to get a bottle of cider from the host of Jamaica Inn on Bodmin Moor in Cornwall, one of the remotest pubs in England, made famous by Daphne du Maurier. The most spectacular was perhaps to obtain a hair from the tail of the tallest giraffe at Whipsnade Zoo. We also had to get a ticket for the Ayr Gold Cup horse race in Scotland (used or unused); a statement from the town clerk in Hungerford, in Berkshire, about the ancient customs of the town; a ring for a teal at Peter Scott's bird sanctuary at Slimbridge in Gloucestershire; a statement from an industrial mushroom grower explaining why the mushrooms he cultivated were grown in the dark; something (I forget what) about arctic exploration from the Bishop of Portsmouth, who had been an explorer; a tail feather from a ptarmigan (winter plumage – summer plumage would not do); and other tasks of similar complexity which I do not now recall. The participants, in my case Michael Pimbury and myself, travelled dressed in denims with no badges of our unit or our rank (we were in any case all riflemen, the lowest form of army life). We were allowed to take one pound only of our own money (no more) and had therefore to rely extensively on hitchhiking at a time when there were very many fewer cars on the road. We started off by being bundled blindfolded into the back of an army lorry and were driven to a place not far from Winchester, but unknown to us, without any maps. It was a magnificent idea enjoyed by everyone from the commanding officer of the regiment downwards. The only person who was mildly uncooperative was the town clerk of Hungerford, who got understandably fed up with meeting three separate teams and lecturing them on the essentially boring local medieval customs. I remember one of these was called Hocktide, which was very much in the Morris dancing category.

Unfortunately, the great initiative scheme turned out to be the last of its kind. The Connington twins, both riflemen and destined for the Royal Fusiliers, had the task of obtaining a hair of the tail of the tallest giraffe at Whipsnade Zoo. This exploit, successfully achieved, got into the local paper and was noticed by the Army Council, who disapproved and decreed that there should be no more exercises of this kind. But the participants had the time of their lives, my brother (and the commanding officer) escaped without a reprimand, and we met a completely new – to us – cross-section of the British public who were generally amused, helpful and generous. One memory is of the team of two riflemen (the winners) who got to John O'Groat's and back without spending a penny and a piece of paper from the station master confirming this. The operation was named 'Lunatics at Large', each competitor carrying a primitive typed card which had some sort of rubber stamp on it, serving as a flimsy explanation for his activity.

People were very kind to us on our exercise. Michael Pimbury and I got a lift somewhere in the West Country from a lorry driver, who took us to a pull-in roadside cafe. He bought us a cooked breakfast (fried eggs and bacon) and refused to take any money or anything else from us in return. A well-heeled couple in their smart Jaguar gave us a lift from the Jamaica Inn on Bodmin Moor as far as Truro. We were cold, dirty, unshaven and smelly in our filthy denims, looking for all the world like escapees from some sort of prison. I remember how the Jaguar couple visibly relaxed when Michael and I confessed to having been at Cheltenham and Eton and were now heading, after our National Service, for Oxford. On the same desolate road on the way back a farmer gave us a lift in his pick-up truck. 'On this very stretch of road,' he said, 'a pheasant flew in through the open window and flapped about on the passenger seat.' 'What did you do?' Michael and I asked innocently. 'I wrung its bloody neck, of course, and drove on,' said our driver grimly, as if this was the obvious, indeed the only, thing to do.

Michael and I probably had the cushiest time on the initiative scheme. The couples who went north to Scotland had a very rough time indeed, it being the autumn and the weather at night very cold. We were all rather pleased with ourselves and glad to have avoided the official rebuke which we were sure would come our way. Instead, the Army Council took a much easier line with us. This amounted to their telling the regiment that 'You'd better not do it again, that's all. You'd better not do it again.'

At the end of two years' National Service in the army you had to join the reserves for a further three years' service with a Territorial Army unit. Mine was called the Queen Victoria's Rifles, a volunteer unit of the Green Jackets. It had distinguished itself in Calais in 1940 when for some days it held up a German panzer force intent upon opening a route for the invasion of Britain. Many riflemen were killed or captured and then imprisoned; and I remember hearing that Anthony Eden, who had served with them in World War I, was said to have felt physically sick when, as Secretary of State for War, he had to order his own regiment to resist the Germans to the last at Calais, and not to surrender.

I joined the Queen Victoria's Rifles as its intelligence officer. Once again, the real and chief attraction was the comradeship of the officers and men in the regiment. Based in London, the commanding officer, a brave, unusual and clever person called Peter Earle, was quick and intelligent but highly erratic, and much given to spontaneous festive occasions, especially those involving the lowest aspects of London nightlife. He was one of my 'referees' for the Foreign Office later on and he clearly made a good impression on the Civil Service Commission for which I was very grateful. This time with the Queen Victoria's Rifles I commanded a very different 'Army of God'. My company commander, Edward Taylor, now a farmer in Cornwall, had the theory that when I wished to summon them I did so by blowing on a conch shell. My sergeant was a ladies' hairdresser from Hounslow who had an interest in introducing me to the girls whose hair he did, showing disappointment

48

when this did not lead to a lasting or even ephemeral romantic attachment. The others were a clerk at the BBC, who I think would have much preferred a more prominent role as a radio or TV presenter; a young man who was a shop assistant in a large London department store; and finally a corporal, who when I last saw him a couple of years ago had become chairman of a successful insurance company. We were a happy band, largely detached from the rest of the battalion, and used our minimal intelligence skills for exercises such as map-reading tours of the Welsh mountain country (the section knew the good pubs in the area).

Then, the fun over, I was posted with my commission as a second lieutenant to Germany, where I stayed for nearly two years, on a large training ground in Westphalia, which the German army had used much for their own training. The British unit next door was the 9th Lancers, which my friend George Ponsonby, with whom I had been in Canada as a schoolboy, joined for his National Service. He and I had dinner together one night – it was quite an early and sober dinner – at my officers' mess. The next morning we set off on our separate exercises, me with the 'Army of God', the eccentric group of riflemen who formed my flame platoon, and George with his armoured car squadron. Halfway through the morning I got a message to say that George's vehicle had overturned in a ditch and that he had broken his neck and was dead. I went to see his mother, Lady Bessborough, who lived very near us in Goodwood and found her sad but composed and philosophical. He was undoubtedly his mother's favourite child.

Apart from the shock and sadness, George was one of those people for whom one could safely predict a successful future. He could have been a captain of industry, a senior civil servant, a bishop – he was a natural leader if ever there was one. His death, and he was only 20 years old, was for me, and his many friends, a major tragedy. To

49

compound it, his cousin Edward Cavendish, who had been another (and naughty) little boy on the *Duchess of Bedford* in 1940 – my aunt called him one of nature's gangsters – contracted polio when serving with the Guards at about the same time. He died, too, after a short illness, thereby depriving the Bessborough family of two of their brightest hopes. It was a terrible tragedy.

My army career ended brilliantly and dramatically. Nearly 40 years after my National Service, I was sitting in my ambassadorial office in Madrid when an ex-army friend telephoned me and asked me with no warning whether I would be honorary colonel of the 4th Battalion of the Green Jackets, who were successors to the Queen Victoria's Rifles. After protesting that I was the least military man he knew and had no knowledge of the modern army, I, of course, accepted, thus making a leap from second lieutenant to full colonel (TA) in a single bound. My duties, I was to find, were light. One was to make a funny speech introducing our guest of honour at the battalion's annual dinner where, in my first year, as the honorary colonel designate, Mrs Thatcher was our guest of honour, and her husband, Denis, a great TA supporter, went to sleep over the soup. The same evening, the retiring honorary colonel, Lord Holderness, read out our routine message of greeting to the Queen twice, before his wife, Diana, exceptionally present, said, 'Shut up, Richard! You did that five minutes ago.' Another duty of the honorary colonel was to attend our annual camp for a couple of days, humiliating myself in the eyes of my riflemen watching me nervously firing machine guns and mortars, the regimental sergeant major carefully photographing and later distributing the (for me) most embarrassing moments. Finally, and more seriously, I had to do battle with Ministers, MPs and officials determined to cut down our numbers or amalgamate, on grounds of economy, with other London TA regiments. The London Irish, for example, with whom we had no common history or tradition and whose uniforms appeared to be covered with feathers and stickers of various kinds, were candidates for amalgamation. The idea was, of course, to save money. The honorary colonel had no duties except to appear from time to time in a fatherly kind of way, and to disappear when not wanted, which was most of the time. The honorary colonels of the regiments concerned met occasionally to discuss possible amalgamation, these meetings arousing in them the worst emotions in terms of regimental pride. One of my opposite numbers, a sympathetic ex-regular major general, said that never in his long career had he heard officers be so rude to each other.

7

The Coronation

Almost exactly 50 years ago while at Oxford I was made, with several other undergraduate friends, a 'Gold Staff Officer'· for the coronation of the Queen; my duties were those of an usher in the royal box for the ceremony and service at Westminster Abbey. This involved taking off three or four days of my term at Oxford for rehearsals, equipping myself with the full dress uniform of the King's Royal Rifle Corps (Green Jackets) of which I was then a territorial officer, attending several meetings conducted by the Duke of Norfolk, and standing at the back of the royal box in case I was needed for anything. I was not.

At one of the rehearsals, Sir Thomas Innes of Learney, the Chief Herald of Scotland, fell in the nave with a great clashing of medals, swords, orders and chains. I rushed to his aid thinking that at last I had something to do, only to find him already surrounded by other ushers and doctors who had got there first. Sir Thomas recovered soon, to the best of my recollection, and seemed in good shape on the day.

At the last rehearsal, everyone dressed up in their robes rather as in the dress rehearsal of a theatre performance. The Archbishop of Canterbury, standing at the high altar, uncharacteristically forgot his lines. 'What do I do now?' he asked the Duke of Norfolk in a voice audible throughout the abbey. Everyone could hear because the duke was standing some way down the abbey in the nave just inside the west door. The duke, a Catholic – indeed the Senior Lay Catholic in the country – said in his special plummy voice, 'You pray.' Another lasting memory is of Lord Mowbray, the Senior Baron of England, doing his homage to the Queen on behalf of his fellow barons (this being the dress rehearsal, the Queen was not present, the Duchess of Norfolk taking her place on the throne). Lord Mowbray, who was quite old, somehow got his baron's robes wound round him like a cocoon, and it took him a little while to unwind himself. While he was doing this and was away from his seat in the abbey, a mischievous peer took his luncheon packet of sandwiches from under his seat – they were in a little brown paper bag there being no food provided by the authorities – and passed them along the pew until it ended up in another row in another peer's hands some way away. On returning to his own seat, his robes finally unwound, Lord Mowbray was much put out and said in a loud voice, which also echoed throughout the abbey: 'Someone has pinched my sandwiches.' His fellow peers feigned shock and horror, and one heard them murmuring to each other, 'How could such a dastardly act possibly have been performed by one of Lord Mowbray's colleagues?' Eventually, after a short but tense interval, the sandwiches were passed back to Lord Mowbray, delivered by a young usher, a Scots Guards subaltern named Angus Ogilvy (later married to Princess Alexandra). He handed the packet of sandwiches back to Lord Mowbray who was only partly mollified. I remember him saying in a loud voice: 'I would never have expected it from a Scots Guardsman.'

My father was present in the abbey also. As the third duke in the land he had the hereditary role of carrying the Sceptre with the Dove in the Queen's procession. My father disliked all ceremonial and hated dressing up and he had a particular problem with the uniform he had to wear. This involved patent-leather shoes with silver buckles attached to them, and he found that he had no patent-leather shoes and no buckles. But my father was an ingenious man, and a craftsman of ability in many areas. He solved the question of the slippers by going to a place in Croydon where you could get a perfectly good pair of bogus patent-leather slippers for £9 a pair. He purchased these and somehow found some old buckles, which he attached to his shoes so that you could not see that any tinkering around had been done with anything. It was ingenious and much admired by all of us. He was greatly relieved when it was all over and he could return to normal life, which did not involve this sort of thing. Apart from him, I had another relation in the abbey. This was a bishop, my Uncle Noel, my mother's brother, the Bishop of Ely, who had taken holy orders at the end of World War I, in which his brother, to whom he was extremely close, had been killed alongside him in the front line. With his DSO and MC, he looked fine in his bishop's robes. He was delighted that I was an usher as it gave him someone to chat to during the occasional intervals we had during the rehearsals. He was in cheerful mood, I expect perhaps enjoying his time off from his episcopal duties. Whenever there was a pause in the rehearsal he and I had an arrangement that we would meet in the abbey's cloisters for a gossip and a smoke.

The only other memorable thing which happened to me as an usher involved the uniform which I was obliged to wear. My friend John Eccles, who was also an usher in the royal box, was wearing an identical one and we each carried a sword which was part of it. We had no idea what to do with a sword when you were in full dress uniform, and certainly not what to do with it when you were walking along. It was therefore to our delight that we heard later that the two senior regimental generals in the abbey – General Sir 'Bubbles' Barker and Major General 'Squeaker'

54

Curtis – had both expressed admiration of the way we had mastered the necessary sword drill. Since neither we nor, I suspect, they had any idea what this involved, I saw they must both have been rather short-sighted. With the uniform and the sword and cross belt and all the rest of the apparatus involved in being an usher, we were each issued with a wand. It was not a very grand one, being made out of wood, painted gold, with blue at both ends, and the royal coat of arms stamped in the middle. I intended, of course, to keep the wand as a souvenir of the day, but somehow I managed to lose it. The circumstances, as I can piece them together after 50 years, involved the chase of a bat round my bedroom at Goodwood House where I was then living. The bat, in a panic at finding itself in the unfamiliar surroundings of a large dark bedroom, swooped around occasionally hitting my head and crouching in places where he was inaccessible to any missile I could throw at him. Everyone knows that the way to deal with a bat is to swat it with a tennis racket. But I had no tennis racket in my bedroom. Another tried method is to turn on the light in the corridor outside your room, turn off the light in your room, open the door, and hope that the bat will fly out – following the light – into your neighbour's bedroom instead. I tried the latter, and the bat flew into the room occupied by my next door neighbour, who I think was my brother, Charles. That was very satisfactory, and I enjoyed a peaceful sleep with no intrusion from bats. The only tragedy was that in the course of my pursuit of the bat somehow the Wand of Office of the Gold Staff Officer had disappeared. It is presumably somewhere in some storeroom at Goodwood, but I do not know where to look for it, so I have lost it; but at least it had some use. Although it had no role in restoring order amongst peers attending the Coronation in the abbey, it drove the bat out of my bedroom.

After the Coronation was over, and it was pouring with

rain throughout, I met Mary, my girlfriend, at some prearranged place on the route and we went with several thousand other people to Buckingham Palace where we joined them cheering and urging the Queen and her family to appear on the balcony of Buckingham Palace. This they duly did, to the accompaniment of more cheering from the growing crowd outside, and the party atmosphere everywhere was very much present. The day ended with my going back to the Eccles' house in Westminster to change back into my ordinary clothes, which I rather regretted as the full dress uniform I had worn all day really looked very fine. But there it was, and the next day I returned to Oxford dressed like an ordinary person with only the memory to accompany me during the rest of my life.

The ushers for the original ceremony numbered several hundred. There was an anniversary lunch party for the survivors 50 years later. Forty-eight people turned up. One was in a wheelchair, and the Queen asked what was wrong with him. 'I was forty-five years old when Your Majesty was crowned,' he replied.

Some other ushers had a more exciting time than me, who only really had to ensure that the German princelings, married to Prince Philip's sisters, were in the right seats, and that Prince Philip's mother, who was more than a little eccentric, was in the place reserved for her. My friend Dominic Elliot, a national service officer, ushering in a peeress's bloc just opposite mine in the choir, had to cope with a baroness, who despite the extremely early hour of her arrival at the abbey, was significantly drunk. I think he got her into her seat in the end.

8

The Foreign Office and Washington

After my military service, and three years at Oxford, I passed the lengthy Foreign Office examination, involving extensive and sometimes eccentric tests, and ending with an interview with half a dozen ladies and gentlemen of the great and good, as they would now be called, including the inevitable lady psychiatrist. We had endless written examinations and interviews, and at one stage, with numbers on our backs like footballers, had to chair a meeting of our fellow candidates designed to resolve some complex problem – to move a university to a colonial territory for instance. The idea was, I suppose, to show an ability to think logically, to display common sense and practical ability and to exercise tact. One of our number got along brilliantly but made rather a mess of the last requirement. One of his committee members, a fellow candidate, questioned his judgement. Instead of listening quietly and tolerantly he shouted, 'Shut up while I'm talking.' I believe the examiners rather liked this unusual approach and passed him, after a little argument, bottom of the list of successful entrants. His career was subsequently very distinguished.

Conditions in the Foreign Office in those days were not good. Grimy offices, coal fires fuelled from ancient scuttles, tall ceilings which were never cleaned in case the cleaning ladies fell and put in an insurance claim, tables used as desks with two telephones on each, one for calls outside and one internal, and loos and washrooms filthy beyond description. I was sent to the American department (Donald MacLean used to be head of it) and, with no preparation and no Spanish, was put in charge of the British relationship with Chile, Bolivia, Peru, Ecuador, Colombia, the Economic Commission for Latin America (a UN body) and a small number of retired British Railway employees who had helped build and maintain the Argentine railway system. They had fallen foul of political change and inflation in Argentina and lived on very small pensions which we tried – with limited success – to increase or at least get paid regularly.

Antarctica, too, was one of our subjects – a problem of great legal complexity. We also dealt with visas for the United States and VIP visitors from our client countries, whom we helped on their visits to London. These ranged from President Elect Kubitschek of Brazil to the all-powerful head of the Bolivian trade union movement, named Juan Lechin. The latter's pretty mistress who accompanied him wanted to know why, if I was a lord, I was working at all. We were reasonably busy but not always. From time to time, when business was slack, the head of the department (an Arabist who knew nothing of Latin America) would summon the three senior members of his staff to his office, lock the door, tell the telephone operator he would take no calls and we would have an agreeable afternoon playing Monopoly.

I had been at the Foreign Office for several months when I received a letter of very smart appearance. It was from Lord (Patrick) Plunket, the Deputy Master of the Royal Household, whose younger brother had been a friend of mine at Eton. Patrick said the Queen would like me to join her party at Windsor Castle for the Ascot Races. I was flattered, pleased and proud. I told my father, who was very fond of the Queen, but, as I have said, disliked formality of all kinds and dressing up. A grey top hat and the other obligatory Ascot wear would be sure to make him nervous and unhappy. His first reaction to my news about the invitation was to say: 'My God, how do you get out of that?' Eventually he concluded that it might be interesting and memorable, and off I drove to Windsor in my little Morris Minor. It was indeed a memorable party and a very posh one. I was in the bachelor quarters, miles away, or so it seemed, from most of the other people staying there. I invariably got lost on my way to breakfast (and what breakfasts!) or to the rooms where the other guests assembled. Some of these were very old and distinguished, some about my own age (I was 23). There were Jocelyn Stevens, Diana Herbert and me – selected I think because we were all friends of Princess Alexandra, who was there for the whole week with her mother and was her usual pretty and jolly self. What made the week unusual was that there was no racing. The railway unions had declared a strike, and train services, on which Ascot depended in those days for its crowd, were all cancelled.

To say that this was a challenge for the Royal Household was an understatement. Fortunately, Patrick Plunket, a person of great taste and charm with a brilliant talent for decoration and party giving, had an instinct for fun and was a friend of hundreds of people including the Queen's own best friends, and he took charge. He had to accommodate almost the entire royal family of all ages and keep in mind the interests of the other guests, and he managed it all with humour and efficiency. One night we had a jolly in-house movie; the next night, the entire party at the castle visited the theatre at Windsor; and the next night there was a ball for at least 200 people, which the Queen much enjoyed – as did I, and I actually danced with her. In the daytime there were other diversions – a tour of the castle, a fascinating visit to its library, a walk around the Saville gardens, and polo and tennis to play and watch. I hit little Prince Charles on the head I recall, with one of my rare ace services. There was much talk and gossip, mostly I confess about people I did not know, and a great deal of horse activity – just no racing, only riding. Everyone was very kind to me, perhaps noticing my state of dithering nerves. The Queen was a marvellous hostess. She had time for everyone and obviously enjoyed herself. The Foreign Secretary (Eden) came to lunch one day (his son was a great friend of mine), and he apparently told the Queen I was doing very well in the Foreign Office, though I don't think he could possibly have known this, even if it was true. But there was always the sense of having to be in the right place at the right time, and there was simply too much to take in, from the wonderful picture collection to the china (a different and rare service was used for every meal) to the food and wine. The sun shone every day.

An extra stroke of luck was the footman called Dickman assigned to me and the other bachelors. He looked after me and the others as if we were the only things that mattered in life. He loved racing too, and for several years afterwards was my guest at Goodwood for Race Week there.

But my chief memory of the week was of the Queen's kindness and tolerance of what I fear must have been a rather boring young man, and of the niceness of her staff, affable, kind and hospitable at all times. Incidentally, there never was, nor is, any shortage of drink at all hours at the royal palaces.

On the last afternoon, I drove down to Oxford, where I stayed in my old landlady's house and attended a party given by the don Teddy Hall. It was one of his more extravagant and uninhibited parties, with massive numbers of pretty girls, gallons of drink and no feeling that you had to behave. I relaxed very quickly indeed myself.

Patrick Plunket tragically died from cancer a few years later. His efficiency and friendliness was matched by his instinct for fun, and no royal party was ever as jolly without him. I remember an older but beautiful lady crying her eyes out in the car-park of the Guards' Chapel, as Patrick's many friends filed gloomily away from his memorial service.

Another friend and ally was the Queen's super-efficient RAF ADC, Squadron Leader Christopher Blount. Having assembled all the guests on the lawn in the castle's main courtyard, he waited for the Queen to join us. We were going on an expedition to somewhere like Frogmore, where many of the royal family are buried. Having successfully got us all together, Christopher said in a loud voice: 'My next trick is to produce the Queen.' As he said it, the Queen popped out of the front door, like the lady who does so in those little Swiss model houses when the weather is about to change. It symbolised the efficiency and effortless ease with which everything at the castle seemed to run.

Then the plan for my future suddenly changed. I do not know where I was originally going, but I was posted to Washington as third secretary and the ambassador's private secretary. I am not clear how this came about. But that was rather the way of the Foreign Office in those days; you were mystified as to how and why decisions had been made.

In those days, you crossed the Atlantic by sea. It took two weeks, but was very much cheaper than going by air because in a ship you could take all your possessions with you for nothing, instead of the two suitcases to which you were limited in an aeroplane. The ship I went on was called the *Media*, which was the only convenient sailing at the time. It had only one class, which was first. It was the smallest ship in the Cunard fleet and had few passenger cabins – I got a lot of attention and service with two stewards all to myself. We passengers, apart from enjoying this luxury, were each allotted a space in the ship's dining room. I had a place at a table for two, my companion being a British exporter in his fifties whose name I forget. In any case, he said it would be best if I referred to him as 'the bald-headed bugger from Woodford Green'.

The voyage took three days longer than it should have done because a violent storm caused the ship to heave to when we were halfway across the Atlantic. When the little *Media* arrived in New York, I was met by Mary, my girlfriend, who had been working there for several months, as a number of enterprising English girls did at the time. She had a job in a florist shop on Madison Avenue, which she obtained after seeking work in many other establishments. She was a trained florist, but in New York the florists were mostly homosexuals and jobs were not obtained easily by females. We spent a day or two in New York before I took the train to Washington. Neither of us had any money to spare, my recollection being that travellers going abroad could only take £25 a year with them. Washington is impressive from the moment you arrive there, from the cathedral-like Union Station to its grand monuments, spacious avenues and the elegant terraced houses in Georgetown.

But before going any further I should include a short chapter about embassies and their functions, a subject of much mystery and misunderstanding in the world outside. Then I will proceed to an account of my first post (as jobs in embassies are called), a life as demanding as anything I had done before.

9

An Embassy

I had better explain what an embassy is and does. In Washington, the British Ambassador of the time, Harold Caccia, was at the apex of an organisation of 300 or so people. Many of them were members of military delegations surviving the war, about half the rest were members of the Foreign Service, and the remainder 'locally engaged' – normally people of English extraction, married or otherwise settled in Washington. The career people included clever graduates, country specialists and experts in technical subjects and were aged from about 25 to 60, when you had to retire. Beneath the pinnacle of the ambassadorial pyramid, there was the Commercial Department – which followed the ups and downs of US commercial policy and assisted British firms seeking to export their products; the Information Department, comprising press officers and others more concerned with writing and broadcasting than reacting to news stories; a large Consular Department in charge of the protection of British (and many Commonwealth) citizens; and, finally an Administration Department. Whitehall has an insatiable appetite for information and advice from the ambassador. Thus, there were in addition, the naval, army and air force attachés and their staffs, a representative of nearly every Whitehall department, and members of the 'intelligence agencies', each working closely with their US opposite numbers. The ambassador had his own personal staff – the demand for speeches and personal appearances was insatiable. At this period a lot of effort was put into holding the wartime alliance together and into collaborating on subjects of mutual interest such as holding the Communist menace at bay.

An ambassador is the Queen's personal representative, notionally (though not in practice) taking precedence over even his own prime minister when the latter is in town, and of course representing his own government. Embassy people work long and hard hours, often in a foreign language, in alien surroundings and in conditions of considerable personal risk to themselves and their accompanying families. Life is not a succession of cocktail parties; drinking champagne with archduchesses, if there are any; the priority is to get as close as possible to the information one needs, to cultivate people with power and influence, and to spread knowledge of and sympathy for Britons as widely as possible. It can be dangerous – two of my closest friends were assassinated by the IRA while serving as ambassadors – but is always stimulating, rarely routine and, for true patriots, which we all were, a real career. There is still scope for individual initiative, and one diplomat on his own can still achieve marvels. I never had a boring moment in nearly 40 years. It is a tough life for wives, but they are as essential as their husbands, above all in making friends and exercising influence.

This is all rather a rich agenda. Some embassies have only two career officers, with all the sometimes heavy and responsible duties outlined above on their shoulders. These people probably have most fun: job satisfaction abroad is very high. At home, work is even harder but the intellectual stimulus greater. The Foreign Service is a *corps d'élite*. I think ours may be the best in the world.

On arrival in Washington, I was met by Charlie Wiggin, a

much decorated ex-RAF bomber pilot, who had joined the Foreign Service after the war and was now the ambassador's private secretary. He was far too experienced for his present job, which I then took over from him, and he went on to something much more responsible and senior. I stayed at his house for some weeks before finding somewhere of my own to live. Charles and his charming wife, Maria, had three little daughters, who were friendly and polite but almost completely silent. I wondered if this was shyness. After a few days their mother said, 'It is all right; I know they don't talk to you but they say they like you very much.' I remember two of the little girls spoke some Swedish as well as English, following a posting in Stockholm, but the youngest spoke no English at all. She had been born in Spain and her first language remained Spanish for some years – she eventually married a Spaniard and now lives in Madrid. Charles's mother was a Spanish *marquesa*, so when Charles eventually became British Ambassador in Spain, he was also a Spanish *marqués*, which caused a certain amount of confusion, but not of the kind that seemed to bother anyone particularly.

Charles Wiggin and I got on well. We both liked baseball very much. Most Saturday mornings after work we would have a couple of dry Martinis at the Mayflower Hotel in Washington and then off to the stadium where the local professional baseball team, the Washington Senators, played – invariably finishing bottom of the league. The team had a cult following of supporters who seemed to derive enjoyment from their lack of success. Eventually, this proved too much for Calvin Griffith, the team's owner, who kept the stadium but sold the team to Minneapolis. Charles and I felt that our fellow baseball enthusiast Dennis Greenhill, who later became head of the Foreign Office, ought to be informed at once. So we sent him a Foreign Office telegram – he was by then in London – rather like the one which the Duke of

65

Dorset's agent sent him in the novel *Zuleika Dobson* to warn him of impending disaster. Our telegram ran: 'Deeply regret inform you that Washington Senators sold yesterday, en bloc to Minneapolis. Regards, Wiggin and Gordon Lennox.' Dennis Greenhill was suitably dismayed, but today the Senators (now called the Minnesota Twins after the twin cities of Minneapolis and St Paul) appear to flourish, even if they don't win many pennants in their northern surroundings.

The embassy was still in the process of adjusting itself to the bruised Anglo-American relationship following the Suez Crisis, at a time when there had been little co-operation and much suspicion on both sides. Harold Caccia, the ambassador, was a clever and energetic senior official, who had been number two in the Foreign Office, and addressed himself to this problem at once. He made many friends and was responsible for a quick improvement in the atmosphere. I was in charge of his private affairs and correspondence. He was a hard taskmaster and taught me a great deal. He was also as tough physically as he had been when he got a rugby blue at Oxford, one of the few old Etonians ever to do so. Incidentally, Harold always wore his old Etonian tie when on his travels. I think this boosted his confidence and made him feel more English, forgetting his grand-paternal Italian origins.

When I did something wrong, or did not do it at all, Harold told me straight, perhaps hurling a file of papers at me as he did so. He had a large, lovely handsome wife who had a strong voice and loved singing and had a robust sense of humour. On one occasion, two aristocratic ladies, well known as spongers, invited themselves to stay at the embassy. They were both talking in Nancy Caccia's sitting room one day and did not see that Nancy was in the room too. One of the ladies said to the other, referring to Nancy, 'How do you find her?' The other lady said, 'I find her enormous and very unfriendly.' Nancy was delighted by this

66

and told everyone. The Caccias had a son, still then at school in England, and two daughters aged about 12 and 17 called Antonia and Clarissa, who were friendly and sympathetic. Antonia used to bully me to do her homework for her.

Another responsibility was the domestic staff; especially Shepherd the butler, a sardonic man with much experience and a dry sense of humour, and an American chauffeur called Hurley, whose pride and joy was the ambassador's Rolls-Royce. He allowed no one else to touch the car and complained a great deal about its mechanics. The chief problem was with the accelerator, which Hurley always called the exhilarator. I spent much time with Hurley, listening to his boring talk about the exhilarator, and often sent him on errands for the ambassador or went with him to meet important people, politicians and others who visited Washington at intervals throughout the year. Sometimes they came with good reason, sometimes simply sponging on the Caccias. Cabinet ministers all seemed to enjoy foreign travel, particularly when this involved staying comfortably with the hospitable Caccias at the embassy.

I travelled extensively in the United States with Harold who in those days had a little RAF plane (a Heron) for his own use, which I suppose was more economical and convenient though certainly much slower than any commercial airline. Together we visited many of the main states, and New York several times, and once the West Coast and a few times the Midwest. Of these trips, the most important and memorable was easily Chicago, a vibrant city full of interesting and very rich people. Mayor Daley, a tough authoritarian and old-style city boss who wielded his power ruthlessly, had given the ambassador an escort of three policemen during his visit. The chief of this little detachment was a Chicago Irishman called Ryan. Beneath him were two detectives of Polish origin, like so many others from Chicago. One was called Klusinski, and the other Semanowski. The ambassador travelled in one car with Ryan, and I was in car number two with Klusinski and Semanowski. They allowed me to work the siren on the police car, which they liked, if possible, to use the whole time.

Ryan, anxious to please the ambassador, asked him if there was anything he could do for him in Chicago. Harold, who had been well briefed, said he had heard you could get very good and cheap lightweight suits there. So our little convoy set off to Franklin Avenue, where these could be obtained. As we drove to the suit emporium, I was still working the siren in the police car. As we drew up at the entrance, a man sprinted out of the front door wearing no coat or trousers and disappeared around the corner. I asked my two police friends what was going on. They said the man was obviously a crook, had broken the law in some way and reckoned that the police siren meant that he had been found out and that the jig was up. Neither cop took this Runyonesque event particularly seriously. I suppose it was the sort of thing that happened fairly frequently in Chicago. We went into the store, full of its lightweight suits. Ryan, a large and burly policeman, was followed by the ambassador, whom he dwarfed. Ryan said in a big voice on entering the building, 'Get me the boss.' Within seconds the boss appeared, another Polish Chicagoan with a tape measure draped around his shoulders. He was a little taken aback and possibly frightened at receiving a policeman as impressive as Ryan. Ryan ignored him and jerked his thumb at the ambassador who was following just behind. 'This here is the British Ambassador,' he said. Ryan paused and then said in a voice that brooked no dissent: 'The Ambassador wants a discount.' Harold, who was careful with his money, was happy with his discount. But I had no money to pay for a suit, discount or not. So I missed my souvenir of Chicago.

Chatting to my two new police friends, I asked them what their normal job was when they were not escorting visiting VIPs. 'Homicide' they both said, and went on to tell me a lurid story of the case they were working on then, which apparently involved the murder of a lady who had been cut up into small pieces, these being distributed in various places all over Chicago, which made solving the crime rather more difficult to achieve. My final memory is of Klusinski and Semanowski visiting, with me, the marvellous Chicago Art Museum. Art was not their strong suit, and at one point I felt I might have to restrain Semanowski from attacking an innocent visitor to the museum to whose general attitude and apparel he had taken exception ('Geez, I could get that guy,' he growled). It was a memorable visit and I parted from my new police friends with affection. It was Mayor Daley, incidentally, who had some hand in manipulating the results of the presidential elections in Cook County, where Chicago was, thus helping Kennedy gain his slender majority over Nixon.

Back in Washington, after staying with and sponging on the Wiggin and then the Muirhead families, I moved into a handsome eighteenth-century bachelor house in Georgetown, then and now the fashionable quarter of Washington. The others there were Tim Guinness, of the KLG sparking plug family and then with the World Bank; Christopher Diggle, a major in the 9th Lancers, who was aide-de-camp to the head of the British Joint Services Mission in the USA; and his successor, Richard Dill, a major in the 8th Irish Hussars. Richard was an accomplished horseman, and past winner of the Grand Military Steeplechase. He was an erratic Irishman with an instinct for trouble and not teetotal. Once a year, a few of us were summoned to a grand house in Maryland, where our much older American host held a reunion for the dozen or so old Etonians in Washington, who included us four. In his car on the way to one of these, Richard said to me, ominously, 'I feel there is going to be an outrage this evening.' He was right. We had all refreshed ourselves on the way. The atmosphere was tense from the start, our first course at dinner being oysters which our host had covered in a pale-blue (for Eton) sauce. Then his wife appeared playing piano accompaniments to Eton songs, which we were all expected to sing. There were audible snorts and giggles from those present. Then our host said he would like to read some poems he had written about his friends killed in World War I. This was too much for Richard, who burst. He hooted with laughter, slapped his thighs, and tears shot from his eyes. It was some time before others present could explain Richard's breakdown, attributing it to some wholly unrelated cause. Richard was an unpredictable joy to share a house with. He was always cheerful, even when hungover, as Irish cavalry officers sometimes are. He sang a lot ('He was a wild colonial boy, Jack Duggan was his name'), and a year or two later married a rich and beautiful Du Pont girl, an excuse for more parties. The marriage did not last, and Richard is now, alas, dead, but the strains of the 'Wild Colonial Boy' still ring in my ears when I think of him.

My job in Washington was that of a 'gopher'. The ambassador would send me to the airport to meet incoming guests if he judged them of sufficient importance, and in that way I think I met every Cabinet minister of that time. Selwyn Lloyd was Foreign Secretary, a man whose temper could be uncertain. He would occasionally telephone me from the embassy residence, which was next door to my office and ask me to do some job for him. One day I was having an ill-tempered exchange with Hurley, the chauffeur, on the internal telephone. There may have been something wrong with the Rolls-Royce, or it may have been another bone of contention between us, perhaps his reluctance to wear his chauffeur's hat. He must have rung me about five times about these matters and I grew impatient. When the telephone rang the sixth time I picked it up and told Hurley to shut up on both matters, and whatever he thought of it he should wear his hat. I used strong language. I failed to realise that I was not talking to Hurley but to Selwyn Lloyd, who was surprised to hear my tone but did no more than gently apologise to me for having bothered me at a time when I was clearly busy doing other things.

Meanwhile, life went on in the Georgetown house I shared. We had many parties there. Georgetown was a small and pretty place, with many friends living in it, and if you wanted a party all you had to do was to go out into the street and gather in the guests, most of whom you knew well. One day Christopher Diggle decided that although there were plenty of parties, there was not enough sex. We all decided to have an aphrodisiac dinner party. We collected four girls, one of whom may have been Jack Kennedy's mistress of the time, and planned an elaborate menu. I remember that we had a lot of oysters and celery, these being recommended by some friend of ours as guaranteed sexual stimulants. The dinner was a great success, but it got nowhere. At a relatively early hour, the four girls, all pleading heavy days the next day, which was probably true, politely said goodnight and went home. We did not try this experiment again, it having proved rather expensive, but we all convinced ourselves that our approach had been sound.

This was all aide-de-camp stuff. My first real job in Washington was to be junior member of a team of three working on a state visit by the Queen the following year. The other two were David Muirhead, later ambassador in Lima, Lisbon and Brussels, and Freddie Leishman, who to everyone's regret resigned to join the bankers Hill Samuel in South Africa, where I hope he made a lot of money. I had a finger in everything: correspondence from members of the public and Congress; security; and visits to Jamestown,

71

where the first English colony was established, to New York for a ball on the last evening, and to Paul Mellon's horse-breeding and -training establishment in Virginia. There were the usual formal engagements at the Capitol and the Episcopalian Cathedral; the opening of the new offices of the embassy, just completed; a huge and chaotic reception for British and Commonwealth citizens in Washington; and of course a banquet given by the President. The Queen carried it all off with good humour, a wonderful example of professionalism which we all admired. Planning was meticulous, and the enthusiasm aroused generated a sort of party spirit, and I don't think I had ever, in my brief career, worked so hard or learnt so much.

The Queen's state visit in 1957 was the first to the USA by a reigning British monarch. It was an extraordinary event with much ceremonial and formality. I was the junior liaison officer with the police and the Secret Service and a general dog's body. We received many letters from the public from organisations such as Daughters of the American Revolution. At least one of them, I remember, insisted she be asked to a reception at the embassy on the grounds of her direct descent from King Edward III. There were other eccentrics, too. One of them wrote to me to say he knew the route which the Queen would be taking in the traditional ticker-tape parade down 5th Avenue in New York. He also knew that a colleague planned to throw his typewriter out of the window which he calculated would strike the Queen in her car on the head. I called Jack Lynch, the head of the police VIP escort department. Jack asked me to send him the letter, which I did. He added in his gritty voice: 'Was the nice guy who wrote this letter kind enough to tell you the building and office out of which his friend was to throw the typewriter?' Jack obviously took this as another little routine problem, but his team was tough and I would not have cared to have been the typewriter's owner.

The Queen came with an enormous entourage. There must have been about 60 people, and I would hate to think how many hands she was obliged to shake. A member of the embassy stood behind her and her husband in the receiving line at the large reception the embassy gave for them: his job was to whisper who the most distinguished guests were. When King George VI did much the same thing on his own visit rather earlier, somewhere down the receiving line was a gentleman who had been a Cabinet minister from an old and distinguished family. Our man in the embassy whispered into the King's ear, 'He is a Biddle.' When he next had a chance the mystified King turned to the embassy man and said, 'What is a Biddle?'

Harold Caccia was an inspired leader, with an eye for detail, and a sharp intellect and keen ambition which carried him forward. I remember someone asked me to describe him briefly, and I said that his instinct remained now as it had been then, as a schoolboy, to get the ball and run hard and fast for the corner flag, heading off opponents trying to stop him. This was an instinct which never left him. For all that, he was a kind person, and I hope I helped him in some way, at least with some of the more detailed jobs he had to do. This was not always a smooth process. Sometimes he asked me to perform some menial task which I forgot. Harold said to me, more than once, 'Nicky, yesterday I asked you to do something for me. What has happened? I will tell you. Absolutely nothing.' It was all very character forming. I wish I could say the same thing about tennis, at which Harold excelled, whereas I found it easier to hit the ball with the handle rather than the strings. After a bit I was not invited to join his foursomes.

The last day of the state visit was a minor personal disaster for me. In the rush to get from Washington to New York I packed David Muirhead's dinner jacket rather than mine. It was several times bigger, David being a very large man indeed.

I had to use various devices including belts and string to turn it into a reasonable fit with my hands kept in my trouser pockets to keep them up. I stayed in the Waldorf Hotel on a floor where Frank Sinatra, in New York on other business, was only two doors away. He had two large bodyguards with him, whose job seemed to be to crack jokes, at which all three would guffaw. Sinatra was pursuing a young woman whom he did not seem to know along the hotel corridor and she was clearly terrified. On the basis of this very short impression, he seemed a coarse and unpleasant person.

The next morning the Queen and her party flew back to England, and we were showered with compliments about the visit's success. There were a number of repercussions. The embassy receptionist said that a well-spoken gentleman wished to speak to the ambassador urgently, no one else would do. Eventually, I persuaded him that I would see him, and pass direct to the ambassador whatever he wanted to say. I met the visitor in our waiting room. He was indeed well dressed and well spoken. He said, 'I am a dentist from Richmond, Virginia. My wife and my friends all think me mad but I am not. I have discovered the cure for baldness. I got very close to your Prince Phillip the other day and noticed that his hair was thinning very badly. But with the application of a potion I have invented it will grow again. Look,' he said and he whipped a magnifying glass from his pocket and we both knelt on the floor, me looking at his scalp through the magnifying glass and sure enough there was a light fuzz growing on his scalp which he said had previously been bald. He had no interest in money or fame, he said, but merely thought that Prince Phillip should know of this secret. I promised to send a record of our conversation at once to Buckingham Palace. Needless to say no one paid the slightest attention. I note that Prince Phillip, now 80 years old, still has a good head of hair.

Harold was delighted that the visit had gone so well. He

told his team of three to take three days off work to thank us. I immediately flew home to England, where I and my girlfriend, Mary, who had left for the UK a little before me, finally became engaged to be married. In my excitement I had completely forgotten that I was meant to have delivered a lecture to (I think) the Daughters of the Revolution on the day of my return to Washington. Fortunately, Freddie Leishman stepped into the breach at a few minutes' notice, and I am told that his lecture, wholly unprepared, was excellent.

*   *   *

By the time we left America we were a party of four – our little baby Sarah, and the extra one being our stern but kindly new nanny, Miss Beachcroft. She was rather older than most of the English nannies in Washington. Before we left, she had a party with the other English nannies, at which they all called each other Nanny, which made it rather difficult to distinguish between them. The party's centrepiece was a large blue cake with white icing saying 'Bon voyage, Nanny!' on it. We left Washington by train. The farewell party which our friends had foreseen at the railway station when we left never materialised. This was because it was election day. Our Democrat friends were elated and not all sober, some of them with the expectation of office in Kennedy's new government. The Republicans, supporters of Nixon, were deeply depressed, suffering from a collective hangover. We all travelled to New York to catch the *Queen Mary* back to England. The US immigration officials, however, said that whereas Mary and I could travel he could not let our baby Sarah go because she had no relevant papers. I had idiotically forgotten to enter her name on my passport before we left. The immigration man eventually softened when we found a British immigration officer on board the *Queen Mary* who took a more flexible attitude.

The journey took a little less than a week and as the *Queen Mary* passed the Isle of Wight and sailed up the Solent we noticed periodic but bright flashes coming from somewhere behind Portsmouth. After a while we guessed what this was and we were right. It was my father at Goodwood. Having checked the time of the ship's arrival he used a large mirror to deflect the rays of the sun so that these were clearly visible on board ship. It was a nice welcome to receive from home. There followed a few hectic weeks in England, and we were off again this time to Chile, where the Foreign Office had decided I would be commercial secretary.

10

Marriage and Children

Of course, the most important of these little essays must concern my marriage. In the early 1950s, I met Mary Williamson at various parties in London and thought her very beautiful and very nice. I subsequently met her on the 6.18 train from Victoria to Chichester (now, alas, discontinued) and discovered that she lived with her parents in West Wittering, only a few miles from Goodwood, where I was myself living at the time. We bumped into each other again fairly frequently, but our next proper meeting was also on a train to Chichester from Victoria Station, this time in the morning and accompanied by my mother. We both decided to visit the dining car, and there was Mary sitting alone at one of the tables starting her lunch and we talked of this and that, mutual friends mostly. It then turned out that to her great embarrassment she had no money, having left her weekly salary by mistake in London, so I paid for her lunch, she promising to pay me back as soon as possible, which she did.

My mother was not pleased. 'You meet this girl whom you scarcely know,' she said, 'and you pay for her lunch because she says she has no money.' This was not a good start to a relationship! As time went on I saw a lot of Mary, and she became what you would call my girlfriend. I rarely went out with anyone else, except in a group. She was working then in a flower shop in the Ritz Hotel in London and subsequently another flower shop in Bond Street belonging to the same firm, which was owned by an immensely rich Irish gentleman called Ambrose Congreve. I spent a lot of time hanging around in both flower shops. I could not make up my mind what to do, being, like most young men, very wary of binding ties particularly those involving marriage, and I felt I ought to start first on building up what I hoped would be my career. Understandably enough, Mary got fed up with my evident inability to decide anything, and after a while very resourcefully took off to live and work in the United States, which in those days was a difficult thing to do. She eventually got a permit to work there and armed with this set out to get a job. She found work with a Mr Tomaino, an outspoken New York Italian whose shop was next to the posh Episcopalian Church in Madison Avenue. The takings for flowers sold to funerals and weddings were particularly good, and sometimes the flowers could be used twice over, once, for example, for a wedding in the morning and once for a funeral in the afternoon. Mary thought this highly immoral and ticked Mr Tomaino off for this illegal practice. Rather surprisingly, although his staff did not like it, Mr Tomaino acquiesced in this moral judgement.

I was still in London, heading for Foreign Office posting to some embassy, I didn't know which, although there was a rumour it was to be Buenos Aires. At any rate, at the last moment the posting was changed to Washington, and when I landed by sea in New York, Mary was there to meet me, which I felt then, and feel now, was pretty loyal considering the offhand way in which I had treated her over our fairly long courtship. I am sorry to say that my tendency for indecision persisted. I got to Washington and started to work very hard, and Mary got herself a new and charming American boyfriend. It was only after the Queen's state visit to Washington in 1957 that things came to a head. As I related earlier, Harold Caccia, the ambassador, was so pleased with the results that the three of us who had worked as a team arranging it were given a few days' leave, to go anywhere we liked, as a reward for our preparatory work, once the visit was over. I decided, for once in my life, that it was time for firm action, flew back to England and got engaged to Mary at Goodwood.

Once back in Washington I broke the news to the ambassador, who recalled that when he had been sent to his own first posting, in China, as the ambassador's private secretary, a firm condition had been that he should not marry. Fortunately, Harold took a contrary view, he having been reminded by his wife that they had both at the time ignored similar advice from the Foreign Office.

While I got on with my work, poor Mary got on with the arrangements for the wedding. This took place, without a snag that I can remember, at St George's, Hanover Square, the church to which the Green Jackets were attached, which had been a fashionable church in the early eighteenth century and was still patronised by very well-off parishioners. My uncle, the Bishop of Newcastle, performed the ceremony, and after a night in Claridges we left for Paris and, after a couple of days, returned to Washington. There we found ourselves a little flat, curiously in the same block where Charles and I had lived with our parents when we were small boys about 16 years beforehand. While I got stuck into working for Harold Caccia, Mr Tomaino was constantly on the telephone to Mary trying to persuade her to come to New York to work for him over the Easter holiday. I explained to him that the ruling then in force forbade the wives of diplomats to take paying jobs, so this could not happen. Mr Tomaino thought this crazy, and said so, and we were both rather disappointed to lose the extra dollars which Mr Tomaino would undoubtedly have given Mary if she could have consented.

We started our family in Washington. Our eldest daughter, Sarah (herself now with four children), was born there in 1960. Apart from the sheer delight of having a daughter, two memories have stuck with me. The first was that, with my wife in labour at five in the morning, I nevertheless had to pay a substantial cheque to the George Washington Hospital before they would allow us in. The second was that, later that same day, I visited Mary and our tiny baby daughter, Sarah. I saw them both through a glass panel, closer access being ruled out for the first day or two. I knew it was Sarah in her little cot because it had a large card attached to it, pink for a girl, which carried the words 'Hi! Dad, I'm baby Lennox.' An authentic piece of Americana with which to embark on life. The doctor was a cheerful gynaecologist, an immensely rich man who owned a luxury yacht on Lake Champlain. 'I'm gonna hit the sack now,' he said after delivering Sarah at 5.45 a.m., and I felt he deserved to do so.

Each of our four children were born in different countries. Our second daughter, Henrietta, was born in Chile. The care Mary received there, and everything else surrounding the birth was quite exceptionally good. The obstetrician was a young Chilean called Dr Gomez. He knew that Europeans sometimes felt that Latin Americans were disorganised and inclined to be late. He promised to be neither, and he was as good as his word. Henrietta was born in an old hospital called the German Clinic in Santiago. Outside the window of her room was a street lined with farm carts which had come from the country that morning, loaded with fresh vegetables and flowers. I always thought this a picturesque way to embark on life. For a while, when Henrietta was actually arriving, I was put in the waiting room with a Chilean expectant father. He was in a terrible state, chain-smoking and with black rings under his eyes. I remember asking him if this was his first child. 'No, no,' he said, searching in vain for an ashtray, 'we have five already.'

When Henrietta left hospital she shared a room with Nanny on the top floor of our little house in Santiago. After a few days we noticed a strong and disagreeable smell in the room, coming from somewhere in the roof. I consulted the Embassy Consul and fixer, a Levantine Chilean Briton called Leo Borax. Leo said we should at once report this to the Ministry of the Interior. I did so and nothing happened. Leo, reconsulted, said we should at once inform the Minister's Permanent Under Secretary. I explained matters to the latter, who ignored the problem of the stink, but was very excited by the news that my wife had had a baby. He congratulated me warmly and kissed me on both cheeks. He promised to send an investigating team. Nothing happened. I returned to Leo. He telephoned the Minister himself and explained about the smell and its ill affects on a newborn baby. He said he suspected that the smell came from decomposing human remains.

This spurred the Chilean police into action. A small squad appeared and proceeded to take the ceiling to pieces. Sure enough, they found a dead cat. They thereby also provided the household with much interest tinged with disappointment that the dead cat had not after all been a human body. Leo was rather pleased with himself. My parents, who were staying with us, were much entertained. Henrietta slept throughout in her little cot.

Our third daughter, Lucy, was born in London, her doctor, and later her godfather, having been a very close Australian friend of mine at my college in Oxford. He was a long time at Oxford, having lost his memory briefly when knocked on the head playing rugby, but we all noticed that he recovered sufficiently to do things like delivering babies, diagnosing his friends' illnesses, and generally enjoying himself. He subsequently became one of the best GPs in London, and his death a few years later was a tragedy for us all.

81

Our fourth child, a son – Anthony – was born in the British American Hospital in Madrid. Dr Mendizabal, the gynaecologist, missed the birth (a Madrid traffic jam?), but he prescribed laughing gas for Mary, which cheered us all up while we were waiting. I think the doctor must have been a descendant of the minister of the same name who shut so many monasteries and convents at the beginning of the last century in Spain, in line with the anti-clerical feeling that was so prominent at the time.

The Church had its influence on Anthony, too. When some years later he failed his Common Entrance Examination to Eton from his private school, we told our good friend the Marquesa de Santa Cruz, the wife of the Spanish ambassador in London and a very grand grandee in her own right herself. She owned several properties in Spain, including a convent which still contained about a dozen elderly nuns. The convent was a beautiful place in a small town called Trujillo (the birthplace of the conquistador Cortes). Casilda Santa Cruz immediately contacted the Mother Superior and told them about Anthony's disaster in the Common Entrance Examination. The nuns got to work at once on their knees, and Anthony sailed through his second attempt, never looking back and was a very popular and successful schoolboy. Casilda was delighted but not a bit surprised and even the storks nesting on the top of the convent tower had a satisfied look about them.

11

Camp David

When Harold Macmillan made visits to Washington (there were several in my time), he was naturally keen on cultivating his personal relationship with President Eisenhower and his team. The two corresponded often, but I always felt that there was something very formal about Macmillan's side of the correspondence, as though it had been worked over (as I expect it had been) by Foreign Office lawyers. The style did not quite manage to reflect the informal friendship which I am sure Macmillan was aiming at. The letters always began 'My dear President' and ended 'With warm regards, as ever, Harold'. These missives would arrive by telegram, to be deciphered in the embassy and sent on their way. The latter was a process which always involved my driving the letter down to the White House in my own car, handing it to the charming Mrs Whitman, who was Eisenhower's personal secretary, and asking her to help me get it to him as soon as possible. This often involved a delivery to a place called Camp David in Maryland, a half-hour's helicopter flight from Washington in a wooded and highly secluded area.

Camp David was a collection of Nissen-type huts rather smarter than the sort we had at home and furnished comfortably inside. The pine trees surrounding the huts provided effective cover from outside observation. The huts were not numbered, but had whimsical names after wild flowers. There was one where the President slept and worked, another for his distinguished guests and half a dozen or more others for the Administration and back-up staff. My job was normally to ferry papers and people from Washington to Camp David and back, and do anything the participants in the bilateral summit meetings may have required or demanded. The whole place had an austere and functional look about it, which went well with the warlike atmosphere in which it had been originally planned. It was, as I said, comfortable, but not luxurious. I did many trips to and from Camp David when there were British ministerial visits to Washington. In fact, I did so many that the United States marines in charge of the Helicopter Ferrying Force gave me a special certificate nominating me 'Honorary Twirlie'. The certificate confirmed that I had made more than a certain number of flights to and from Camp David and was signed by an impressively senior marine officer. What was more remarkable was that the text was typed in Gothic lettering. Somewhere in the Pentagon then was evidently (and probably still is) a lady using a typewriter with Gothic lettering, which must have been a rarity then as it is now. I wonder if she still has the machine upon which the certificate was typed. Like most good things, I expect this has vanished with time. I also wonder whether the lady who designated me an 'Honorary Twirlie' had other jobs to do in the Pentagon. I hope so, but I shall never know.

The helicopter crew who ferried me to and from Camp David consisted of a pilot, co-pilot, and, in the small passenger compartment with myself, a very tough-looking sergeant in the Marine Corps. I wondered what his job was – perhaps something to do with safety or a technical job of some kind. My friend Norborne Robinson, an American who had been in the Services, said that the sergeant was in the back of the helicopter in case one or more of the passengers lost their heads and became hysterical, in which case he would

84

have rendered them unconscious with a single blow, at the very least. Afterwards, I always looked on my companion in the helicopter with a certain trepidation.

12

Sir Winston Churchill

Towards the end of my time in Washington, Winston Churchill, encouraged by his friend President Eisenhower, decided to make a last visit to the United States. There was nothing official about his visit. He came as the President's friend. Churchill stayed in the White House, which allowed me to inspect the premises. It is a comfortable rather than a grand house, and I remember bouncing on the beds to ensure they were not too hard. There is material about this visit in Mr Gilbert's massive Churchill biography, including some of the letters I exchanged in advance with Churchill's private secretary, an ex-Diplomatic Service officer and friend of mine called Anthony Montague Browne.

Mary and I went to Washington Airport to see Churchill arrive from New York in the 'US One', the President's personal aircraft, which in the photograph I have of his arrival looks ancient and decrepit. As its doors opened, President Eisenhower, despite his own years, ran up the aircraft steps and embraced Churchill just as the latter appeared at the door and escorted him down to the tarmac. There were short speeches, a guard of honour and a band which played the national anthems, and then the two drove away. Everybody watching was greatly moved. A few days later I received a photograph of the event, signed by President Eisenhower, who sent it to me via his charming secretary (and incidentally, wife of the President of the American

Fruit Company), Mrs Whitman. It was one of Mary's and my best memories of all our years in the Foreign Service.

Being so junior I scarcely got near the great man, who was by then very old and spoke very little. A group of us at the embassy, however, had a brief word with him when he returned from a day out at President Eisenhower's farm in Gettysburg, where he had been driven around in a golf buggy. There was a silence when Churchill returned to the embassy until some brave person asked him about the Gettysburg visit. 'How many cows were there?' the person asked. Churchill gave him a precise answer. 'And pigs?' Churchill replied, 'I do not know. They did not allow me to see the pigs.' There was the slightest tone of disappointment in his voice, and I discovered later that Churchill had an affection for the animals and was disappointed at not having seen them.

There was a banquet in the embassy on Churchill's final evening. I still have a list of those who attended it. Apart from the President and his Cabinet members, they consisted nearly all of generals involved in the war and others associated with them. Most of them arrived in smart limousines, chauffeur-driven. The exception I particularly remember was General Mark Clark, by then retired and head of an army academy in the southern United States. When he left, he strode out into the night unaccompanied, except by me, for his walk home, resisting all my attempts to suggest a more comfortable journey. He was a fine figure of a man, immensely fit and strong with a gentle and courteous manner even towards the smallest form of life at the embassy.

The next morning Harold Caccia accompanied Churchill to the airport, with me sitting alongside Hurley in the front of the Rolls-Royce. Hurley had his hat on, but was still muttering about the performance of the accelerator. Churchill said nothing for a while until, addressing the ambassador, he said how grateful he was for the visit. He added: 'I hope you will give the Prime Minister (this was Harold Macmillan) a good report of me and say that I behaved myself.' It was a touching occasion. Most of us knew that we would never see Churchill again. The only crisis, if you could call it that, was that Churchill managed to cut his finger. The British doctor attached to our military delegation was summoned and dealt with it. Because of Churchill's great age it might, I gathered, have turned into gangrene. It did not, and the doctor asked for a photograph of Churchill to remind him of the event. I remember the rest of us were all very stuffy about this and reckoned that a small cut on the finger did not deserve a signed photograph from the world's greatest statesman – he never got one.

13

Beecroft and Macmillan

Beecroft must have entered our lives after the war when my mother hired him as a temporary butler for a number of years during Goodwood Race Week. I was in Washington at that time. Aldridge, the temporary butler until then, had been dismissed for, among other things, pinching the gin – an expensive item, rare during the war and post-war years. Beecroft must have been in his seventies, with snow-white hair and a polite and respectful disposition.

Before his retirement from regular employment, Beecroft had worked as a valet and butler for F.E. Smith, Lord Birkenhead, the great friend of Winston Churchill. According to his own account Beecroft had one day called Lord Birkenhead at the usual reasonably early hour one morning to find His Lordship enraged, accusing him of stealing his gold watch, which he, Lord Birkenhead, had in fact given Beecroft sometime before as a token of his gratitude for his services. Beecroft eventually explained matters to the satisfaction of Lord Birkenhead, who accepted reluctantly that he had been wrong. 'His Lordship was of course quite drunk at the time,' Beecroft explained.

Macmillan never came to the Goodwood Races, horse racing not being one of his interests, but he did come to Paris several times when we were there in the 1970s. Meeting him was a problem, as he had a tendency to topple over when making his way down the tube-like escalators to the ground floor at Charles de Gaulle Airport. Once I got him back to the embassy, he entered the lift to go to his room on the top floor, observing that he and Pat Hancock, his private secretary some years before, had got stuck in the lift when they last entered it. No sooner had he said this than the lift got stuck again. Macmillan was happy about this. 'There!' he said, pointing to some scratches on the door of the lift, 'You can still see where Pat tried to release us with his penknife.' Eventually the lift got going again, and we went along to his bedroom where he read me the text of the speech which he intended to deliver that day to the Cercle Interallié, a smart and prestigious club next door to the embassy, after dinner.

We (the Anglo-French dinner guests) took our places at the table awaiting the arrival of our guest of honour. Then Macmillan entered the room on the arm of his grandson and promptly dropped all his speech notes, which scattered all over the floor. After a brief introduction by the club president, he began his speech in hesitant French (we were expecting it to be in English). He dropped a few more notes and after getting his grandson to find them again on the floor, he re-embarked on his speech in his halting French. We were all embarrassed, English and French alike. People did not quite know where to look. Then he dropped all pretence and delivered his speech in eloquent English to the relief of all of us (the French present understood every word), receiving a standing ovation at the end. It was a deliberate and masterly ploy, that guaranteed a successful and interesting evening for all.

I saw him once use precisely the same technique when he was chairman of the Beefsteak Club, myself being a member of his committee. He managed to instil a feeling of apprehension in his audience, who thought that he might be seriously ill, and certainly incapable of delivering a coherent speech. But he recovered himself in no time and with the same result as he had achieved in Paris. In a strong voice and scarcely using his notes, he delivered a speech which those present will long remember. It was a brilliant technique – the relief at his recovery being accompanied with delight at the humour and eloquence of the speech itself.

The next time I saw Macmillan for any length of time was when he visited Washington in the course of a short trip to dePauw University, a small and charming college in rural Indiana with a high academic reputation. The connection was via his mother, Indiana being her childhood home and native state. What I had not realised – we were all very busy at the time – was that in addition to his private secretary, typists and policemen, Macmillan had brought his now elderly (and still temporary) valet, Beecroft, with him.

When I went to Washington Airport to meet Macmillan and his party en route for his various engagements and for Indiana, I scurried about in my usual way collecting passports, hand luggage and seeing the visitors to the cars allocated to them. I had just about finished this menial but essential task when a voice behind me said: 'Good morning, my Lord, and I trust you have good news of Their Graces?' It was, of course, Beecroft, ancient but cheerful, happy to receive a good report on my parents, to whom he was devoted. I rather think this was the last time he accompanied Macmillan on his travels. This was not on account of his age, but because of some near-Wodehousian drama about Macmillan's socks for which Beecroft bore some responsibility. He had not pinched the socks, like Bertie Wooster's temporary valet, but I think some had gone astray. Still, it was a memorable occasion, and I think Beecroft had a happy visit. But I think he felt rather more at home at Goodwood than he did in Washington, or at a provincial American Midwest university.

14

Chile

In 1960 (it was in fact the day of Jack Kennedy's election) we were posted back to London, with our next destination Commercial Secretary in Santiago, Chile. About half a dozen of us from the Foreign Office were sent on a course to learn what a commercial secretary did. The course was not a particularly good one, and we were not good learners. It did, however, take us to places in the United Kingdom we had never visited before. In addition to the City of London, we spent some time in Liverpool and Bradford and other places where we might reasonably hope to learn something about the exports we would be seeking to help promote. One of our number, who much later became ambassador to Italy, wore a bowler hat, as many people did in those days. It was the first time he had done so since his last foreign posting, in Bolivia. It looked pretty absurd in Bradford, but apparently much more so in Bolivia, where he had been the object of derision because bowler hats were things worn by women and not men.

We stayed in hotels, which the Foreign Office seemed to have selected for their cold and cheerless lack of comfort. Every industrial plant we visited, and we went to many, insisted on showing us their blast furnaces. These are things that once you have seen one, you have seen them all, and after a while we made it a condition of our industrial visits not to visit places where we were once again exposed to the sight of molten metal being poured out of buckets. In the City, we spent some days with the banks, particularly the old National Provincial. Two things in the City left me with a lasting memory. One was the discount houses. The directors, all 'gentlemen', arrived sometime in the mid-morning, ate a copious lunch and left at about three o'clock in the afternoon, leaving the business in the hands of a few young exchange dealers, who in effect ran the business and made the money, which was considerable. We also spent some time with commodity brokers who dealt in all sorts of products. One of the most important of the latter was, it seemed, rhinoceros horns, which they imported from Africa to sell to the Far East, where they were highly valued as aphrodisiacs.

Our journey from England to Chile in 1961 was on the SS *Amazon* of the Blue Funnel Line, a relatively modern liner. It took us first to Cherbourg, Vigo and Lisbon, and to Rio, Santos and Montevideo, and thence to Buenos Aires. It was a memorable trip on which we tried to improve our Spanish through an excellent small book called *Teach Yourself Spanish*, which I would recommend to anybody embarking on that language. The senior passenger on board was unquestionably the Earl of Beauchamp, with his lively but elderly Danish wife. The captain of the ship asked Lord Beauchamp to make a speech at a gala dinner which took place during the voyage. Lord Beauchamp did this, but seemed a little vague as to what was required. His chosen subject was gas pipelines, a topic of mild but not overwhelming interest to the remainder of the passengers. Despite its irrelevance, the audience did not seem to mind and Lord Beauchamp duly received his applause, which appeared to delight him. This was followed by the inevitable fancy-dress ball, into which Nanny threw herself enthusiastically. She dressed as a pirate with a black patch over one eye, thus limiting further her short-sightedness. She was normally practically teetotal, but helped herself liberally to the ship's red wine. The next morning she arrived late at our cabin, complaining of a headache and an upset tummy. 'It must have been something you ate last night,' I said, this being something I had always wanted to say to someone.

During the voyage, the weather was beautiful and warm, and we swam a lot in the swimming pool. There were a number of nice people on board, and when we got to Santos, which is near-tropical in climate, we decided to make an expedition into the interior, to São Paulo, which is a city unlike any other I have seen – enormous, chaotic and noisy. It was a very hot day and humid and not at all the kind of day you would have selected for making an expedition into the interior of Brazil away from the coast. But Lady Beauchamp, who wanted to show us some jewellers, was quite firm. We hired two taxis and soon found ourselves in São Paulo opposite a large building called H. Stern, the foremost jewellers of South America and, looking back on it, a posh establishment. We were exhausted, hot and sticky, and our tempers were not even very good. We were placed in a waiting room, where a glamorous Brazilian lady appeared and asked whether we would like a drink. Most of us settled on a gin and tonic, which appeared in a matter of seconds. The glamorous lady said, 'I am sorry for the delay. Mr Freddy will be with you in a moment.' Mr Freddy duly appeared – a wonderfully suave salesman, beautifully dressed and with a carefully trimmed moustache. He was, of course, multilingual and within minutes had sold us some lovely pieces of jewellery, including a large pale aquamarine which Mary still wears very frequently. After another gin and tonic, we left and, in a much better mood, drove back in our taxis to Santos. By then there was a light tropical rain, and I was intrigued to notice that all the dockers carried umbrellas.

Then on to Montevideo, which, during a brief visit, I found to be a charming old-fashioned little city. A few hours later we were back on board, sailing across the Río de la Plata to Buenos Aires where we disembarked. I remember the customs people in Buenos Aires giving us a bad time, not necessarily because we were British, but because they were bloody-minded. Eventually we were cleared and went to stay the night with Richard Parsons, who was destined a few years later to be my predecessor as ambassador of Madrid. He was one of the most amusing of my colleagues, and I wish we could have stayed with him longer. But we were soon off again, this time travelling to Santiago in Chile by air. It was a spectacular flight which took us through the Andes, the aircraft often flying level with the summits of the highest mountains, which marked the boundary between Chile and Argentina. On arrival in Santiago, where the embassy was a relatively small one, we found, after some days there, two small service flats in the Avenida Bulnes – one for Mary, Sarah and me, and one for Nanny. There ensued a difficult several weeks in which we searched for a house to rent, which were in short supply in Santiago.

Eventually we found ourselves a little house several miles north of the city. It belonged to the daughter of a gentleman called Tony Gandarillas, a notable international society figure who was I think on the fringes of the circle of Edward VIII and spent much time in Europe, as many well-heeled South Americans did. There was just enough room for us all to squeeze in, and a pretty garden for the children to play in. A few days later, after a delay which allowed the Chilean customs ample time for searching and pilfering our possessions, which they did with enthusiasm, our things arrived in huge packing cases, on each of which was my name and destination printed in large letters. Not long after our arrival in our new little house, a horse and cart arrived, driven by a Chilean with a marked resemblance to one of the seven dwarves. He had somehow noticed our, by then empty, packing cases in the customs and did a deal with us by offering to buy them from us. We closed on a price and later on heard that he had wanted the cases for his family to live in (although he said he wanted them to house his animals). Somewhere in the foothills of the Andes there may still be a crude residence, originally one or more large packing cases, with a Chilean family inside it (and Chilean families are not small ones) labelled 'Lord N. Gordon Lennox, British Embassy, Chile', as though it had been a house in the West End of London. I hope it is still there.

Chile in those days was a stable and tranquil country with a small but active middle-class community dependent upon trade of all kinds but especially exports of copper. Few Chileans were very rich compared with many people in other Latin American countries, but the vast majority lived near the poverty line, many in shanty towns (known locally as *callampas*), and to all intents and purposes outside the national economy. These were a mixed lot, largely descendants of different invasions into Chile at the expense of the Araucanian Indians, whom the Spaniards had subjugated some years before, in the later years of the nineteenth century. Mixed in with these were the descendants of immigrants from the Basque Country in Spain. There were also colonies of English, Scottish, Welsh, German and Palestinian (whom the Chileans called '*Turcos*') settlers, who had arrived there to trade but had decided to stay, marrying Chilean girls and producing large and usually beautiful families.

The country itself was spectacular – if it was nearer Europe we would all try to go there for our holidays. The eastern boundary was the immensely impressive Andes, snowcapped throughout the year and so tall it seemed to blank half the sky. The climate was gentle, the wines delicious, and the women beautiful. At least, this was what

Richard Sykes, the number two in the Santiago embassy and a close friend of ours (later murdered by the IRA when ambassador in The Hague) told us to say when the Chileans asked what we thought of their country; and certainly it never failed to go down well. Chileans, furthermore, had an instinct for democracy and the ability to laugh at themselves. Wine was cheap and consumed in vast quantities, even by the poorest. The Chilean cockney, traditionally poor and ragged, was known as a *roto*, meaning literally a 'broken one', and it was usually wine that had done the breaking.

There was always a certain unreliability about the workmen you employed. My own experience was that plumbers in particular belong to a guild whose chief characteristic appeared to be their addiction to drink. Once when our boiler burst, we found one who installed a new one for us, but not without difficulty. He was stripped to the waist because of the heat, sang a lot and was rarely sober. When the boiler was finally started up the water in the house was freezing cold, but scalding hot where it was used on the flower beds in the garden. But the chief characteristic of Chile was undoubtedly the vast and tall mountain range of the Andes, second only in the world to the Himalayas. It surrounded Santiago, thickening the pollution which in any case was to be found everywhere else in the city, in the summer or winter. After we had been there a few days, Mary asked somebody in Santiago where these mountains were, she could not see them from the street. The answer was she simply was not looking high enough – if she cast her eyes upwards she would see their snow-covered peaks.

Much of my work in Chile involved travel to the north, particularly to nitrate fields, fish-meal plants and copper mines, which, we hoped, would buy British machinery. Sometimes our machinery was very good, but not always as good as that made in the USA and other European countries, and Chile, being desperately short of foreign exchange, had imposed what was virtually an import prohibition. If you wanted to sell something good in Chile, the best way was probably to smuggle it in. This state of affairs made me a temporary expert in mining machinery, fish-meal and, of course, illegal consumer goods. It involved me also in extensive journeys to the Atacama Desert, visiting the mines – mostly copper ones – staffed by people from many different countries. I soon discovered that these mining communities were most interesting places. The technicians and engineers, mostly from Europe and the United States, got on very well with each other and were good employers of the vast numbers of Chilean labourers working under them. My work also involved visiting small Pacific ports, previously centres for exports and imports, but now sadly run down and deserted.

I spent some time, for instance, in the small town of Coquimbo, where the elderly honorary British consul was a kind of supreme arbitrator. There were very few strikes in Coquimbo. If the unions and management disagreed, they normally trooped off to see our consul, an expatriate Scotsman in his sixties or seventies called Don Victor Goudie, who sorted matters out for them. Then there was Iquique, a sadder and smaller place which had once been the centre for the nitrate business during the latter's boom years. It had a big nineteenth-century bandstand in the middle of its main square and a huge English Club with one of the biggest bars in the whole country. There were now, however, very few British or, indeed, any kind of members. The most prominent was undoubtedly our honorary vice-consul Mr Steven Coy, who had once been in the nitrate business himself. He and his two elderly sisters formed the core of the community, which in the early days had been a large one. Now, with the discovery of substitutes for nitrate, Iquique was no longer the boom town that it had been, when you had to queue at the bar for some time in order to get a drink. Mr Coy was a charming old gentleman and took me to see the principal people and places in Iquique. Our first call was on the mayor and local authorities, Mr Coy enjoying a short but clearly refreshing sleep during my talk with the mayor. I asked him about the rest of the British community in the city, and he said that there were now very few. 'Mainly,' he said, 'my two sisters and myself.'

I subsequently met his two sisters at a party he gave for me, where there were a few other British subjects, mostly retired, present. The sisters were jolly ladies much at home in Iquique and happy to receive an actual Englishman there. When I asked them when they had last been home they replied that they had never been home. 'Steven' – the vice-consul – 'was at home once, but we never went there.' Nevertheless, England was still home to them and whatever news they could obtain about it was of great interest. They talked English with the slight but charming sing-song accent common to many Anglo-Chileans, and I remember them as being well-dressed and hospitable hostesses, and their party – although on a modest scale – as very enjoyable.

Another port I visited from time to time was Arica, in the extreme north of the country. My American colleague said that if Chile had an enema, Arica would be the place where they would put in the tube. It was a collection of small import/export businesses not unlike Andorra, which I got to know later, and where there was plenty of merchandise on display in the many little shops, but nothing you wanted to buy. Arica had an Anglican church constructed out of cast iron, many little businesses selling whisky and cigarettes at knock-down prices, and a genial and amusing ex-RAF British honorary vice-consul, with a friendly and spirited Anglo-Chilean wife who subsequently took over his job. It was on the border of Bolivia and Peru with many commercial and, I suspect, illicit trading deals taking place between the three. My last sight of the amiable vice-consul, whom I visited several times, was his falling backwards into the hotel flower-bed as we parted after a particularly jolly dinner.

The President of the republic at the time was Don Arturo Alessandri, a conservative and elderly bachelor, much respected, who seemed to be permanently dressed in a white tie and tails with a sash of the Office of President, red, white and blue (the Chilean colours), round his middle. A nervous man, his psychiatrist (I was told) advised him to drive his own car to and from his office every day, presumably on the grounds that if you could tackle the daily traffic in central Santiago life would no longer hold any terrors for you. This was possibly effective in calming his nerves, or was it just a rumour of the kind that used to circulate in Santiago? A colleague of mine at the embassy, however, driving home one evening found himself immediately behind the President, alone in his own limousine, shakily preceding him in the usual Santiago traffic jam to get in and out of the city.

I met Salvador Allende only once – he was related by marriage to an Anglo-Chilean family. In the summer, he used to take a house in a little fishing village on the coast called Algarrobo, next door to one which we would borrow or stay in occasionally. People like Pinochet, who was in the news in Britain a couple of years ago when he was arrested by a Spanish court order, were unknown in social or public life. Indeed, as far as one knew, the army played little or no part at all in national politics. The navy, almost indistinguishable from our own in its traditions and even its mannerisms, had a number of second-hand British warships, and two smart new destroyers (made by Vickers) which did not always work perfectly. The air force was entirely American-influenced, most of its pilots having received their training in the United States. The army's activity seemed to be occupied to a great extent in public works and other non-belligerent activity. In its appearance it seemed to look to the Germany of a bygone age. It looked smart (especially its ski troops in their white uniforms), it wore German army helmets and did the goose-step on formal occasions. The role of the armed forces in Chile when we were there was the exact reverse of in Argentina and other countries only a few miles away across the cordillera of the Andes, where military governments intervened from time to time when it became clear that civil dictatorships were failing in the tasks they set out to perform.

I would not say that my time in Chile was wholly useless, although the ban on imports certainly made it difficult for businessmen to sell in the market. They (the visiting British businessmen) varied greatly in quality. In some areas we did good business, and one firm gained what turned out to be the virtual monopoly in the sale of compressors from England. There was also a constant supply of exports of spare parts for the Royal Naval vessels, which the Chileans had at some stage purchased from us. The immensely long Chilean coastline made it necessary to deal with marauding Argentines or smugglers from Argentina or other areas.

On one occasion, which was not untypical, a British exporter turned up in my office, unannounced, to say that he wanted to make inroads into the Chilean market with the roasted, salted peanuts his firm manufactured. I told him as gently as possible that imports of consumer goods like roasted, salted peanuts were prohibited and that he had anyway arrived in Santiago on a public holiday when all offices and shops were closed. He was not in the least deterred by any of this. Two days later he turned up again to say that he had succeeded in capturing a majority share in this business. So I had the pleasure of eating his roasted, salted peanuts at the best hotels in Santiago. I have no idea, to this day, how he wangled it.

There were two additional memorable events in which I played a humble but useful role in Santiago. I was there

101

for the arrival of the English football team for the 1962 World Cup. The ambassador took little interest in them from the start so I was the person who went to the airport to meet and welcome them. I found the team a nice bunch of boys with a cheerful approach. I can remember most of their names (but hope I may be forgiven if I have forgotten one or two). They were led by the polite and urbane Haynes (then with Fulham) and included Bobby Charlton, Armfield, Wilson, Robson, Peacock, Douglas, Norman, Greaves, Stiles and the appropriately named Ron Springett, the goalkeeper from Sheffield Wednesday. They played well but not brilliantly and eventually fell to Brazil, the final winners, in a later round. I went to all their games, and to others too. At one match between Argentina and England, the crowd rose and cheered for several minutes when England took a 1–0 lead. For one heady moment I thought that we were really popular in Chile. The real reason, of course, was that the Chileans disliked the Argentines and vice versa, and as elsewhere in Latin America there was surprisingly little contact between the various nations or their inhabitants, who generally had offensive names and gestures for each other which they did not hesitate to use on any appropriate occasion.

We gave the team and their accompanying officials a party at the embassy which they seemed to enjoy. Mary got on particularly well with the charming Bobby Robson (now a Sir). The team and its officials must have nearly outnumbered the visiting fans from England, for whom the trip from home must have cost a fortune. I remember an RAF sergeant in his uniform, on leave, who had somehow managed to come from England and a genial gentleman wearing a complete Union Jack ensemble – socks, trousers, waistcoat, jacket, top hat and even umbrella. He cut rather a lonely figure in the stadium among the thousands of Chileans and supporters from elsewhere, but at least we were spared any trouble from football hooligans, as there weren't any. There cannot have been more than a few hundred of mixed nationalities in the crowd, packed into the little stadium at a town called Rancagua, about 50 miles to the south of Santiago. I was sorry to see the England team lose against Hungary in the first round, largely because they were such nice and well-behaved people. But I think the climate and the altitude and the generally unfamiliar conditions were very much against them, and I know they did their best.

Another wholly different and more solemn duty of mine involved the Oyster Research Centre (of which I had hitherto been unaware) in Colwyn Bay in Wales. This was after many of our own oyster beds had been destroyed in the storms of the early 1960s, and a young scientist from the Colwyn Bay Station had been sent to Chile to see if the Chilean oyster beds could be transplanted in some way to the North Sea. I met him at the airport, and he had a suitcase with him containing specialised equipment to assist his investigations. The Chilean customs, ever diligent and suspicious and certainly not above bribery or pilfering, got the idea that these were instruments for procuring abortions. I disabused them of this (to me) rather mad suspicion. The young man from Colwyn Bay, by now unhappy and much affected by seasickness and the change in climate, set off for the south to see the Chilean oysters in their natural habitat and came to the embassy in Santiago before returning home to Wales. I thought I had better report to the ambassador, who had now taken some interest in the proceedings, and found him quite curious about them. He said, 'Er, Nicky, how do oysters sort of "set about it"?' I knew the answer then and explained it to him, but have forgotten it now. The ambassador and I jointly concluded that whatever the oysters did they derived little fun from doing it. Anyway to our disappointment, although delicious, they were found unsuitable for transfer to our own beds in the North Sea and areas round the United Kingdom.

Nanny had, of course, a distinctive role in Chile. Apart from her friendship with other English nannies, most of whom were now rather ancient, she had a number of special friends, one of whom, with his wife, serviced the tote at Santiago Racecourse. Nanny used to visit them often and watch the races, and so did we. The standard of racing was surprisingly high. There were many good horsemen in Chile, and polo players too. Prince Philip once visited Chile when we were there to play polo, my chief memory being his irritation at some aspect of the game played in Chile which he felt was incorrect or inappropriate. Nanny would return from these expeditions to the racecourse by bus, a considerable distance and a trip not undertaken without risk, as Chilean buses were ancient and mechanically unreliable, the passengers or driver were not always sober, and Nanny spoke no Spanish. However, I do not recall an occasion upon which the bus driver did not drop her down at exactly the right place, near our house, and she enjoyed these expeditions.

13

Back to Britain

From Chile, after nearly three years, we were posted back
to London. I was again to be private secretary to Harold
Caccia, replacing Douglas Hurd. Harold Caccia, meanwhile,
had been promoted from Washington to be head of the
Diplomatic Service, with two years to go before he became
provost of Eton, and a non-executive director of a number
of companies which paid him good fees (we added these
up and they totalled a very comfortable sum for someone
living in the 1960s). He was as sharp as ever and I struggled
to get to the office before 9 a.m., when he did, but not
always successfully.

By then our family had grown. There was Mary, myself,
Sarah and our little baby Henrietta and, of course, Nanny.
We travelled in a liner called the *Reina del Mar*, the flagship
of the now defunct Pacific Steam Navigation Company. The
journey took three weeks. We travelled with all our possessions,
which we could take with us without charge, and our three
weeks' journey did not even count as leave. We stopped at
many places on the way back, starting in Valparaiso, and
stopping on the way at Callao, Cartagena, La Guaira, Aruba,
Caracas, Trinidad and thence across the Atlantic to Lisbon,
Vigo and Southampton. Then there was the usual fancy-
dress ball, at which I regret to say I appeared as a 'Baby
Doll' after the lady in the film. I can remember myself and
another new friend (this time an English expatriate working

in Peru) getting mournfully drunk at the ship's bar before the frightful celebration began.

Once back at Goodwood, I confessed to the customs agent who interviewed us that I had bought well over 200 bottles of Chilean wine with me. The duty I paid was modest, some of the wine had not travelled well, but the rest kept us going for some months. We received many presents from generous Chilean friends, including some goat's-hair slippers which smelt so strongly (of goat) that we threw them out of our porthole while we were still moored in the harbour at Valparaiso.

After we had been back in London for nearly two years, Harold Caccia retired. He was succeeded by Paul Gore-Booth, the ex-High Commissioner in Delhi, a devout Christian Scientist with poor eyesight, which without a strong light amounted sometimes to near total blindness. He was a good, kind and patient person, but lacked Harold Caccia's toughness. He had a charming and beautiful wife, Pat. One of his sons, David, joined the Foreign Office and in his turn became the British High Commissioner in India.

The office of the head of the Diplomatic Service was served by two elderly Foreign Office messengers. The senior of these was Mr Page. One of his duties was to announce the arrival of foreign ambassadors who were calling upon Harold Caccia or Paul Gore-Booth. Mr Page would first usher them into my office, so that I could introduce them formally. Once Mr Page opened the door and announced the arrival of the Ethiopian ambassador and, with ancient memories of the famous racecourse tipster Prince Monolulu, added in an audible undertone, 'I've got a horse.' His deputy, Mr Chapple, had for some years been a driver of the number 11 bus, before the days of bus stops. If you wanted a number 11, and you saw one approaching, you waved it down, and it stopped for you. Or I am certain it did if driven by Mr Chapple, he being one of the most courteous people in the Foreign Office, of any rank or age.

After serving a while as Paul Gore-Booth's private secretary, I swapped jobs with Patrick Wright, the Polish Desk officer, where I read with fascination the frequent and hard-hitting sermons of Karol Wojtyla, then Archbishop of Kraków – outspoken and brave and later on to be Pope John Paul. I never wangled my way to Warsaw, which I still regret.

Following this I was posted within the Foreign Office to be chairman of the Current Intelligence Committees (a group of meetings), designed to assess the dangers from (short-term) threatening trouble spots and report our conclusions as soon as we could (within the day if possible) to ministers. Ted Heath read our reports, I know, because we could sometimes decipher his signature or comments on what we had said. Other ministers read them too. They were usually very brief, and they gave ministers a short updating on problems they were likely to be asked about. We reported through my immediate superiors, who were a couple of ranks higher than me, and full members of the Joint Intelligence Committee. One of these was John Thomson, an extremely clever member of the Nobel Prize-winning family, and later Percy Cradock, ambassador to China. I was lucky with them both. Their brilliance was acknowledged within the Foreign Office where they wielded great authority.

Every Whitehall department with an interest in intelligence matters was represented on my committees. One colonel from the Defence Intelligence Staff of the Ministry of Defence (MOD) would arrive with his much more knowledgeable number two, who would stand up when he had something to add and, addressing his colonel (not me, the chairman), say 'Permission to speak, Sir?' Another absurdity was that our superior body, the Joint Intelligence Committee, always met regularly once a week, when the current intelligence problem we were dealing with had been analysed and – for our committee at least – been dealt with. Thus, to my knowledge, the JIC never looked early enough, if at all, at the Falkland Islands problem. If they had, the war might have been avoided, or at least the British government would have got better warning of the serious trouble ahead. There were, of course, other factors at work too, but this lapse, it seemed to me, was one of the worst of the post-war bureaucratic omissions until the affair of the alleged Iraqi weapons of mass-destruction which do not seem to have existed.

There were some grim moments, but not all that many. Once, at a weekly JIC meeting, I made a mild joke about a presentation I had just given. A genial colleague from the Ministry of Defence (he was the expert on Africa) sent me a piece of paper which said 'No jokes'. After some months in the job John Thomson sent me for three weeks to India, Pakistan and Sri Lanka. The war was just beginning whereby East Bengal hoped to gain independence from India. The Muslim Bengalis from what was then East Pakistan were being harassed by their opponents who were actually seeking to prevent this. In Bengal, I spent some time with the Pakistani freedom fighters (called the Mukti Bahini), who were delighted to show me the spot where mortar bombs had landed the previous night, and did not seem in the least disturbed by the possibility that more might land now, effectively ending our discussion. I also visited many refugee camps in Bengal, to the north of Calcutta, where literally millions of Muslim refugees from East Bengal were housed in primitive conditions, in camps guarded by the Indian army and cared for by Indian nuns.

I drove into one camp with a colleague from our High Commission in Calcutta, to be surrounded by a menacing mob of refugees, most of them undernourished and all with a message to get across. The leader of the mob, a refugee from East Bengal, acted as spokesman for the others. He appeared extremely angry, and I took it that his complaint concerned lack of food and other essential necessities. Not at all. As an East Bengali, what he wanted was not food but an intellectual exchange. He said, 'I should like to exchange impressions with you on the world situation,' and he meant large subjects such as world peace and not minor affairs such as the impending war between Pakistan and India. I reported to the Foreign Office on my return that war was inevitable, ending with the independence of Bangladesh. I also had something to say about the refugee camps and the efficient organisation of the Indians, civil and military, who ran them. The most pathetic sight was a large ward for the little Bengali children; each had a camp-bed with a relation – perhaps a mother or a cousin – looking after them. But some were orphans, both parents having been killed in their flight from their homes into the relative safety of India. Some of the orphans were very small indeed. There was one little more than a baby lying on her camp-bed, looked after not by her mother, who had been killed, but by her seven- or eight-year-old sister, who had taken her place.

I also made some calls on officials in Calcutta. One was the chief minister of Bengal, an Indian who was the effective boss of the city. I thought I would get a broad view from him on the present political situation and its prospects. Unfortunately our conversation was interrupted seven times by his telephone ringing. Six out of the seven times, it was the wrong number.

A final call was on the chief of police in Calcutta, a youngish and intelligent man who wanted to know if I was an admirer of Hegel. I, in turn, asked him how he had dealt with the violent terrorist group in Calcutta called the Naxalites, whose menace seemed recently to have decreased. The chief of police said this was a very sad affair. Many of them had tried to escape from prison and were shot while trying to do so. I resolved then that it would be a good idea to keep to the right side of the law in Calcutta. When I returned to

London, John Thomson was pleased with my report, which I sent to Number 10 Downing Street and I think it may have been read by Ted Heath. But the Foreign Office experts on the Indian subcontinent were not entirely happy. Although my conclusions were not far from their own, it was clear they resented an outsider having trespassed on their territory.

16

Foreign Office Spokesman

For something under one year thereafter I was Foreign Office chief press officer and head of a department of eight or so press officers, each one in charge of an area of the world or a specific subject. Dennis Greenhill, the head of the Diplomatic Service, appointed me. I always felt he was a little optimistic in how his appointments would turn out. This was no exception. My appointment was not an unqualified success, but I improved with time. It took me some while to realise that journalists needed really good information if they were to do any kind of job, and I must be free and relaxed in briefing them. Every morning, I held a formal press conference with the diplomatic correspondents of British newspapers, radio and television. In the afternoon I and my press officers would usually give each of them a one-on-one unattributable briefing. For traditional reasons, *The Times* man always got preferential treatment. I liked this, because I liked *The Times* man; but the days of the diplomatic correspondents had by that time been overtaken, and it was rarely that he got anything of significance published anonymously or over his name. Specialist journalists had generally taken over from the diplomatic correspondent for whom the world was their oyster. This tendency seems largely to have been reversed, and foreign affairs corres-pondents now seem more numerous.

My other duty, or rather the main one, was to accompany

the Foreign Secretary on his travels and to speak in his name where required. I soon found out that the diplomatic correspondents were by no means all alike. Some were genuinely expert and knowledgeable, some lazy and dim. Some were conspiracy theorists, notably the current Press Association man. Some were convinced you were lying to lead them astray. All of them were in some degree neurotic, this being caused by their insecurity of tenure and their occasional inability to understand the issues being discussed. I once gave a briefing to a quite well-known reporter for a Sunday broadsheet. When a day or two later, his piece appeared, it was entirely contrary to what I had told him in matters of fact as well as interpretation. I reached for my telephone and asked him to call me as soon as possible. I then told him that he had wholly misreported me; I wanted to develop a relationship with him in which we could trust one another in future, and I hoped he wanted to do so too. To my amazement and distress, he started to cry, saying his mother had always brought him up to be a boy who told the truth. I think our contact was a little bit easier after that but never free of an undercurrent of tension.

Then, when Alec Douglas Home, the Foreign Secretary, went abroad, I was nearly always with him, whether the party was small or large. Sometimes it included only a hard core: Antony Acland, his private secretary and later ambassador in Washington and permanent under-secretary, and Miles Hudson, his political adviser, an amiable and clever Hampshire farmer with strong political views. A lot of our time was spent in Brussels, sometimes at NATO meetings but more often at meetings of the European Community (as it was then called), the venue varying from time to time according to the country which held the Presidency. There was usually some sort of crisis to discuss, rarely soluble. In the oil crisis of 1973, all the EC foreign ministers met in a private meeting to discuss the way ahead. After a while we learned to our horror that all or nearly all of the foreign ministers of Arab countries were on their way to Copenhagen with a view to joining our meeting and presenting their case in person. This they did, at immense length. No officials or advisers were allowed at this meeting, we were all waiting outside the conference room for a snippet of news which we could pass on to the press and the outside world. Eventually, after a long wait, the doors opened and the ministers emerged, blinking as they came into the light, and the meeting at last seemed to have come to an end. Alec was among the first to appear from it. I asked him what had happened and what I, his spokesman, could tell the press about it, there being a dozen or so journalists in various states of intoxication waiting in my hotel room to get their copy for the next day's British papers. Alec, the gentlest and most tolerant of men, merely said to me, 'Where is the nearest synagogue? I want to become a Jew.' I did not feel that this quote would create quite the right tone for the headlines in the next day's British press so I made up something more anodyne for them: a pity, because I think they and many others would have enjoyed what Alec said.

The climax of my activity as the spokesman and head of the News Department came when Ted Heath's 'three-day week' was accompanied by a series of crises which led to the 1974 general election. A summit of the European Community heads of government took place, to discuss pressing European Community business, but Ted's permanent press officer, Robin Haydon, was detained in London to deal with the serious domestic political problems which had arisen. As Foreign Office press officer, I stepped in and took his place at the summit. I saw Ted only infrequently the next day – his meetings were held in another part of Brussels and I and the press for some reason spent much time seeking him in the wrong place. When I did see him at the end of his working day, my job was simply to find out from him what I could tell the British press corps about what had taken place. I explained to him that I had 20 or so correspondents waiting and, of course, drinking in my hotel room to hear what Ted had to say. This group were the notoriously difficult lobby correspondents, who differed from other journalists in that they had special access (or thought they had) to Number 10. Some were offensive, the *Daily Express* man particularly, until I noticed that he had a Schweppes tonic-water bottle balanced apparently permanently on his head, rather diminishing his dignity. The lobby were idiosyncratic and were far more interested in making speeches than listening to my answers to the questions which they put to us. To brief myself in advance I asked Ted a lot of questions, and he was extremely laconic in his answers. He mostly said 'Yes' or 'No', which did not give me much to go on in briefing the press.

Anyway, Ted said the meeting had gone quite well. I remember one serious concern at the time was for the health of Willi Brandt of West Germany. 'I found Willi in quite good form,' said Heath. Again, scarcely headline material for the British dailies. The lobby correspondents continued to orate, and I did my best to answer them. The upshot was a wholly chaotic British press the next morning, confused, sometimes contradictory, and often sensational. It was no help at all to Ted in his election campaign, correctly giving the impression of a great muddle. When, some months later, we met at a meeting in Paris and he was in Opposition, I asked him if he remembered my role as his temporary spokesman at the summit. All he said was 'I remember'. When, later on, I asked Robin Haydon, his permanent press officer, how he dealt with a situation like this, he said he (Robin) usually made the answers up himself as he went along.

Easily the best informed group of our journalists and the

most intelligent was the small group of mostly young men in Brussels covering NATO, European Community affairs, and the business of the other multilateral organisations based there. I learnt far more from them than they did from me. After a long and tedious ministerial meeting in Brussels one weekend, where EC foreign ministers had met to discuss that most arid of subjects, regional policy, I gave a long and boring briefing to the journalists about what had happened at the meeting. Eventually I ground to a halt and told the correspondents that I had told them everything I knew. 'Yes,' said the young *Times* man, 'we can all see that.'

Our small team made other trips. One was at a time when the Soviet Union was under Brezhnev, although he was in poor health. Our rather large British delegation arrived at Moscow Airport late at night, and I was housed in an old-fashioned hotel which had a bathroom which you approached through the corridor. Tired, I undressed quickly and sprinted to the bathroom to see if the water was hot or not. It was not. Twice more I sped there to see if the water had heated up and after a little while discovered it had. It then occurred to me that in order to get to the bathroom I had had to approach it through a little corridor which had glass walls on either side. If a KGB photographer had been sitting behind the glass walls of the corridor, he could have obtained good footage of me running naked between the bedroom and the bathroom; it would not have been much trouble for him to juxtapose me with a nubile Russian lady, providing him with a welcome piece of blackmail. This would not have required much ingenuity, but the photographer, if indeed he was interested, seemed not to have realised its potential. I did not quite know whether to be disappointed or not.

We spent three days or so in Moscow talking to Russian ministers and officials. There were a number of issues need-ing discussion (however sterile), as there always were with the Russians in those days, from disarmament to the Middle

115

East; and Alec in any case wanted to meet some of the Russian hierarchy (in the end he had to be content with Podgorny, who was very much a stand-in for the more senior ministers, who, it was said, were not available). Gromyko presided over the Russian team at the talks, and when these ended we took the night train from Moscow to Leningrad. We were accompanied by several extremely high-spirited members of the staff from the Russian foreign ministry who drank all the vodka they could lay their hands on during the night journey. They pressed us to keep up with them in this, and Antony Acland, Alec's private secretary, said he had the feeling that the Russians were looking at us closely, hoping to discern character weaknesses which could be used at some later stage against us. I had a very bad cold, so anything I could have said on that occasion would have been incoherent and no use at all to the KGB.

The short visit to Leningrad was deeply moving. It took place in the freezing cold in a heavy snowfall, and we spent some time visiting the memorial where very many Russian victims of the German siege in the 1940s were buried. It was, for me, a very Russian occasion – with the biting cold and the all-pervading feeling of gloom and melancholy, accompanied by mournful military music – which brought home to us all the atmosphere of the siege and the appalling losses and privations suffered on both sides. It left a profound impression in my mind which did not leave me for some time.

Then we spent the best part, in fact much of the next day, at the Hermitage Museum, with its unequalled collection of paintings, ancient and modern, housed in the palaces which had been built by the Tsars of the past. There were wonderful things to see there, far too many to remember from a single short visit. Our motorcade then drove us to the airport to fly back to London. On the way, Gromyko suggested that we took a look at Leningrad's ultra-modern

The author with his mother and older brother Charles, 1934.

The author, his brother and others en route to Canada on board the Tiddly Quid in 1940.

A letter written from the author to his parents from West Montreal.

The author, painted by Olive Snell.

The author and his contemporaries at an Oxford dinner in 1952. Nicholas Gordon Lennox is second on the right of those seated.

Mary aged 21, photographed by Lord Snowdon.

Painting at Norton Hall with Winifred Clemence Dane, the author, Sandy Llewelyn and Anthony Hornyold, 1952.

The author at his wedding to Mary, London 1958.

Goodwood House - The Family Seat.

Photograph © Goodwood Collection.

Winston Churchill and Eisenhower on Churchill's farewell visit to the U.S.A. Author (background) was private secretary to the British Ambassador Sir Harold Caccia, May 1959.

The author and Mary meeting Freddy and Betty Richmond on their visit to Santiago, 1962.

The author and Mary meeting the Spanish classical guitarist Andrés Segovia.

Lucy with her sisters Sarah and Henrietta at her christening in Chelsea Old Church, January 1966.

The author presenting his credentials to the King of Spain on his appointment as HM's Ambassador to Spain, July 1984.

Norman Blacklock, Bill Heseltine, Ginnie Airlie, the author, Mary and Richenda Elton on board the Royal Yacht during the Queen's State visit to Spain, 1986.

Nicko and Mary Henderson, Paris 1979.

The author and Mary with the Count of Barcelona, the late father of the King of Spain.

Mary and the author with the King of Spain aboard the Royal Yacht during the
Queen's State visit to Spain in October 1988.

'Dammit Juan Carlos! Don't you put your clocks back in this country?'

The author having a picnic with his friend Peregrine Pollen in a field near Toledo, 1987.

metropolitan railway. It was indeed modern, with a glistening new train standing at the main platform in the station. Its only curious feature was that there were no members of the public about, at a time when there ought to have been crowds. We drew the conclusion that the would-be passengers had not been allowed to enter the station or board the train until the VIPs had been given the chance to admire this example of Russian modern technology. We had a merry trip in the empty train as far as the next station. Alec actually drove the train himself, which we all rather enjoyed, and we got to our destination in one piece. The Russian I chiefly remember on that trip was the Mayor of Leningrad, a very large middle-aged lady, with a big moustache. She talked a little English and was highly critical of the, to her, large sums of money you had to pay in London to attend such events as the theatre and concerts. (I remember that I said that I rather agreed with her.) The visit 'went well', as these visits of this kind are usually destined to do, and the British press corps in Moscow who were with us were knowledgeable and friendly. One of them was an old gentleman who had been one of the Invergordon mutineers at the close of World War I and had somehow escaped to Russia to avoid punishment at home and had stayed there and settled down. He crept up to me at one stage during a reception and asked if we might have a private word. We moved to a corner of the room, and, dropping his voice to an undertone, he said to me, 'I have some important information for you. They are arming in the south.' I have no idea to this day what he was talking about but promised I would report it immediately when I returned to London.

Before we left we were all given presents. Mine was a samovar, evidently for decorative purposes only, as the lid and spout were both blocked in, making it unworkable. The Foreign Office security people suggested they examine it in case it had a listening device hidden within. I never got around to taking it to them, which enabled me to continue to suspect that it did indeed contain some device (it made and still makes a rattling noise when you shake it) and that the KGB people listening to the messages it transmitted would get a gabble of conversation from my children.

I think everyone enjoyed the visit to the Soviet Union. Not everyone had been there before, the intense cold and driving snow making Moscow appear just what we all felt it ought to be like. It was quite a success for me, too, and I remember Julian Bullard, the Foreign Office's chief expert on Russia, telling me that he thought that thanks to my briefings the press had produced the right kind of reporting on the visit. It may, of course, have been that he was merely being polite.

A few weeks more of press conferences in London, routine affairs followed, and then Alec decided that he wished to make a visit to Africa, where he had not been for some time. This was a moment of high emotion over Rhodesia, and the idea was to talk to the leaders in four countries – Zambia, Malawi, Tanzania and Kenya – to explain our point of view and to see if there was any room for agreement with them over what was fast becoming a serious crisis for the British government. The trip was a qualified success.

The Zambian visit was relatively free of incident. It was a hot and humid day when the Zambian President, Kaunda – a man given to emotion – wept a little on receiving Alec, whom he had got to know before at various conferences in London and the Commonwealth. Kaunda and Alec had a long talk, sitting at the end of an immensely long dining-room table. Kaunda's ministers and our little party were ranged on either side of the table, and it was difficult for them or us to hear what was going on between the two principals. Some of Kaunda's ministers, bored with the proceedings, passed the time making bread pellets and flicking them at one another.

118

Malawi was a totally different matter. It smelt of the dictatorship of Dr Hastings Banda, who had been in charge there for a very long time, having many years before started his career as a GP in England. My first sight from the aircraft window as we landed at Lilongwe, was of a smartly uniformed policeman beating up, none too gently, a spectator who he evidently judged had strayed too far onto the airfield. A big dinner in the open air, with a military band, ended the day. My great regret was my failure to obtain one of the lapel buttons, worn by each of Dr Banda's ministers with a portrait of the doctor on each, with the words 'Long Live His Excellency the Life President' surrounding the portrait.

Tanzania was different again. As our aircraft landed at Dar es Salaam, I was working on an amiable speech for Alec to make, declaring his pleasure in being in Tanzania again and at the prospect of talks with the President, Dr Julius Nyerere. As the aircraft came to a halt the pilot said over the intercom: 'I am afraid there is no question of anyone leaving the plane at present. The airfield is crowded with hostile demonstrators who will need to be cleared to make a path for you to get to your cars.' So we sat and waited for something to happen, and I reflected on the futility of my little arrival speech.

Eventually our High Commissioner arrived, and he announced that he had persuaded the police, who appeared to be working hand in glove with the mob, to clear an exit path to our cars. We walked gingerly through what must have been a hundred or so protesters all shouting angrily about the British role, which they believed to be in support of the status quo in Rhodesia. Many carried placards with offensive or obscene messages written on them. One unusually tall and well-developed Tanzanian carried a large placard declaring in big letters 'Motherf*****s go home'. We eventually reached our car (I accompanied Elizabeth Home) and set off, with the 'Motherf*****s go home' man running alongside the car beating the roof and continuing to shout his slogan. Eventually at the airfield perimeter we shook him off and drove to the High Commission where we restored ourselves immediately with large whiskies.

The next day began with talks between Alec and his Tanzanian opposite number. The day was hot and humid, and the room airless. The minister droned on about the iniquities of British policy towards apartheid and the United Nations. Meanwhile, our team noticed to their consternation that Alec's eyelids were becoming heavy and closing. But before we could decide what action, if any, to take, the minister mentioned the British diplomatic attitude towards apartheid as this affected the forthcoming Olympic Games. Alec showed every sign of waking up at this point. 'Minister,' he said, 'you have mentioned the Olympic Games. Last night, when we arrived by air' – he was too courteous to mention the hostile reception we had received from the demonstrators at the airport – 'there were a number of people with placards shouting at us and one of them ran so fast we only just shook him off at the airport exit. He was shouting the whole time and hitting what you would call a nice easy pace which enabled him to keep up with the car. If you can find him, and train him up a bit, I think you will find him a very good prospect for Tanzania in the 1000 metres in the Olympic Games.' As the Tanzanians showed absolutely no sign of understanding this, the subject changed again and Alec's eyelids again began to droop. When, on my next visit to Paris, I saw my colleagues at the Quai d'Orsay again I told them this story and they were delighted. 'We wish we had a foreign minister like that,' they said.

Our next and last stop was Nairobi, or rather Mombasa, where Kenyatta and his closest ministers were awaiting us in his sumptuous seaside villa. He was wearing a short-sleeved shirt of multicoloured Hawaiian-type design. His huge arms were decorated with thick gold, jewel-encrusted bangles. He spoke slowly in his deep bass voice, and there was much courtesy on both sides. The rough words were reserved for Kenyatta's number two, Arap Moi, sitting at his boss's side. 'Are you looking after my friend Sir Alec, Moi?' Kenyatta enquired with more than a hint of menace in his voice. 'Are you doing everything he wishes?' It was very much a one-man act. The other members of Kenyatta's team kept quiet. Our feeling was that no one dared interrupt the great man. 'Now that you are here, Sir Alec,' said Kenyatta, 'I hope you will stay for some weeks.' Alec explained gently that he had to get home very soon indeed (in fact, the next day) for the forthcoming general election campaign and could not at this stage take up Kenyatta's offer. After a while, Kenyatta appeared to accept this with good grace.

I remember asking Alan Campbell, who was in the party and who had been Foreign Office spokesman some years before me, if there were any tips he had about how to deal with African journalists. 'Yes,' said Alan, 'three. First, speak very loudly and slowly. Second, get them to write down as clearly as possible what you have said. Third, if you can, read what they have written when reporting you in their little notebooks.' This worked well enough, but not absolutely always.

After the 1974 general election, which the Tories narrowly lost, I began to wonder what this would involve for me. I learned soon enough. Harold Wilson was now Prime Minister and James Callaghan Foreign Secretary. My late boss, Alec Home, was out of office altogether. I got a message from Callaghan's office shortly after the election results saying that he wanted to see me urgently. I duly went to his office and noticed that his private secretaries were less jolly than usual. I sat down and Callaghan told me that he was dispensing with my services. I knew he had already got rid of our ambassador in the United Nations, and I knew also that Robin Haydon, the Number 10 chief press officer, had been sent packing too. I was evidently the third to go. Callaghan said that the fact that he no longer needed me had nothing to do with who I was, or what my performance was; it was just that he had had his own press officer for many years and wished to keep him with him now. This was Tom McCaffery, a loyal friend of James Callaghan, a good man and a thoroughly professional and experienced press officer. Before I could say anything, Jim Callaghan started to say more about his plans for moving me. After explaining his close attachment to Tom McCaffery, which he did not wish to break, he promised to find me a good job in the place of the one I was now to leave.

Before I left him, he said he wanted to say two things to me. One was that he wanted my journalist friends to know that the Labour Party, which had announced that they intended to renegotiate the terms of our entry into the European Community, had every intention of doing so in good faith. Second, he asked me whether there were any particular points he should bear in mind when speaking to the press about the Middle East. As to his first point, I had a sudden picture of my journalist friends questioning the phrase 'in good faith' and left his office very relieved that I would not have to explain to my contacts what 'in good faith' meant in practice. I could imagine some of the things they would have to say. As to the Middle East, I said that the world would be watching everything and that any deviation from the tried and accepted formulae about the Middle East crisis and how to set about improving it would be noticed and criticised. I suggested he take very detailed advice from the experts in the Foreign Office on how to handle this.

We had chatted for about an hour, something which I have always regarded as a generous gesture from someone who had only just been appointed as Foreign Secretary. We parted good friends and have remained so ever since. He came to stay a few days with us a few years later when I was in Madrid. For some days after being dismissed by him, I decided to be awkward and refuse any new job offered to me, partly out of bloody-mindedness and partly because the job of head of the News Department was one of the best in the office and I could not think of another one likely to replace it in terms of importance or quality. I hung on for a week with no job to do, which I found an agreeable experience. During this time Mary and I decided to have a party, which we all enjoyed. Eventually, Mary told me it was about time I took a decision about my future and stopped being awkward.

She was, of course, right, and I decided to accept the job on offer, which was head of the North American Department. This was a very small unit, but it had one or two important jobs to do. One was following and explaining in Whitehall the complicated twists of the Watergate scandal. Another was coordinating and writing the main briefs for talks with Dr Kissinger, who was still America's Foreign Secretary. The briefs covered international problems all over the world, and my education was much enhanced. I sat in on several talks with Dr Kissinger and his entourage. At the end of each session of talks the two foreign ministers would ask their advisers what they proposed to say to the press about the meetings which had just taken place. I recited to the meeting what I had in mind to say, only to find Dr Kissinger glaring at me. 'Vy do you not say that our talks were constructive?' he asked. 'My talks are always constructive.' I promised to take account of this when I eventually briefed the press, and everyone seemed happy thereafter.

A little later, I travelled to Wales with Dr Kissinger and Callaghan, when the latter was about to receive the Freedom of Cardiff, which was in his constituency. He thought that this would amuse Dr Kissinger, as well as giving them the opportunity to talk during the air journey to Cardiff and back. So, with a little help from my friends in the American Embassy, I travelled from London to Cardiff in Dr Kissinger's aircraft. Occasionally he looked at me menacingly as if to say, 'Who is that guy – get him out of here.' But then he was pretty tough with his own staff too, let alone strange foreigners. His wife, however, was charming, and we later spent a happy hour purchasing English 'candies', which she professed to adore – the cheaper ones such as toffee and Mars bars being the ones she liked best.

I survived the journey to attend the large and grand dinner at Cardiff Castle in Dr Kissinger's honour, at which the guests after dinner all joined in a Welsh sing-song, a moving, unexpected but, I am told, not infrequent occurrence. The two principals both spoke wittily and well, but both were upstaged by Lord Tonypandy, who had been Speaker of the House of Commons, and whose strong and lilting Welsh accent captivated the whole audience, English and American alike.

17

Paris

My next job was in Paris, where I was 'Head of Chancery' – an archaic title which really meant chief of staff to the ambassador, the latter being my old and close friend Nicko Henderson, who was a delight to work with. The French, by contrast, were not easy – at least the middle-range and middle-aged officials with whom I had to deal.

We lived in one of the gatehouses of the embassy residence, almost in an annexe to the embassy office. To get to and from work, I walked through the embassy kitchen, where I observed the chef at his labours; he must have been among the best in Paris. When I looked out of our bedroom window across the courtyard, I could see the ambassador's feet sticking out of the end of his bed. My US opposite number said, 'The head of chancery should be near to his ambassador at all times, but that is ridiculous.'

It was not a particularly happy ship; it was too large for its real needs, but was generally staffed by people of real ability. I had a few good friends at the Quai d'Orsay and some others who had nothing to do with the diplomatic work of the embassy.

The best moments were when we travelled out of Paris, where life was less tense and formal. But I was stuck in Paris most of the time. My conclusion is that the French capital is a posting either for the younger diplomats with little or no serious responsibilities, or for the great and the

125

good and senior people. For sheer beauty, though, Paris has few equals in the world.

The Queen Mother visited France privately nearly every year, and three times in different years when we were in Paris. Once she stayed at the embassy, the other times in large and grand chateaux. The routine followed the same lines. At the French end, the organiser and master of ceremonies was a wonderfully amusing elderly gentleman called Prince Jean ('Johnny') de Faucigny-Lucinge, who was also the uncle of Madame Giscard d'Estaing. He was very fond of the Queen Mother, but told me once he was running out of suitable chateaux for her to stay in, and that, after several visits, the job of organising them was very probably killing him. Certainly the expense incurred on both sides was immense.

The Queen Mother's visits were preceded by a reconnaissance party consisting of a saloon car driven by a chauffeur, with Sir Ralph Anstruther, an ex-Guards officer until recently the master of her household. This was followed a little later by another vehicle containing a detective, her private secretary (Sir Martin Gilliat), a young army ADC and a lot of luggage and several cases of gin. The gin was for presents for her hosts and consumption by the royal party itself. Her hosts gave elaborate lunches or dinner parties for her and arranged for her to see the most interesting local sights and meet the most interesting local people. They were always delighted to receive her, despite the burdens this put on them, particularly since her visits were not undertaken alone. She normally came with friends such as the Duke and Duchess of Grafton, Lady Diana Cooper, and others. Her French was still pretty good, and her curiosity was insatiable and she never appeared tired. Nights were always late ones. In Paris, she visited the main exhibitions and was entertained by old friends. She had a banquet one evening given by the ambassador.

One year, the embassy team planning the Queen Mother's visit, which meant myself and Howard Davies, then the ambassador's private secretary (and now director of the London School of Economics), decided to take her out to lunch. But where, we wondered, would be suitable? Eventually we settled on an excellent but traditional restaurant at one end of the Place des Vosges. Howard and I went to take a look at it. The menu looked excellent; there was a large alcove at the end of the restaurant suitable for our party of about 12; and the proprietor, I was delighted and relieved to see, had the Légion d'Honneur in his buttonhole. He understood at once what we wanted and appreciated that royalty very much liked going out to restaurants, as they only rarely got the chance of doing so, and choosing what to eat and drink themselves, rather than having an elaborate set banquet placed in front of them.

The Queen Mother much enjoyed it all. 'What a lovely time we are all having!' she said, and she had a chat with the proprietor before walking to her Rolls, which was waiting outside for her. It was surrounded by small French children, to whom she also chatted for a while before returning to the embassy, driving through a small, friendly and applauding crowd. I had incidentally noticed that although the restaurant was full, the other people there for lunch hardly even looked up when our large royal party came in. My strong feeling was that to avoid the press and ensure a degree of privacy, the super-discreet proprietor had arranged for the other diners, or at least the occupants of nearby tables, to be members of the French equivalent of MI6.

In Paris, I was also a sort of administration-cum-political officer, with duties that included acting as the liaison between the Windsors, who lived there in their old age, and the courtiers at Buckingham Palace. The Duke of Windsor had died in 1972 but the duchess lived on, comatose and bedridden, until 1986. I had met them both earlier on a short trip to Madrid and Washington, but I never saw them in Paris. They lived in their house in the Bois de Boulogne, and sometimes I went for a talk, which included tea, with their lawyer, Maître Blum, who was elderly, aggressive and highly litigious.

I never quite knew where the Maître's unwavering loyalty to the Duchess of Windsor came from, but of its existence there was no doubt. She was a self-appointed guardian to the duchess, in cooperation with Henri, the butler, and her doctors at the American Hospital in Paris. Guests and callers, even old friends, were not admitted to the house. The fact was that, at least according to Maître Blum, the duchess had only moments of consciousness, a sad contrast to the lively, energetic and amusing person I had met in earlier years. She had the gift of putting people at their ease, and her delight in social occasions communicated itself to the people around her. I never quite knew how ill she was, but I suspect she had only brief moments of lucidity during the day. Maître Blum looked after her every need.

Maître Blum professed profound admiration and respect for our queen, but the rest of our royal family was beyond her contempt. She reserved a special loathing for Mountbatten, whom she accused of removing some of the Windsors' possessions, of real or sentimental value, while the poor duchess lay unconscious in bed. I always suspected that there was some element of truth in this. Maître Blum was quite sure about Mountbatten's alleged activities, and her vituperation against him knew no bounds.

Anyone who suggested that the Windsors had slept together before marriage, moreover, would find themselves at the wrong end of a legal process conducted with no quarter. Her husband, a general from the Franco-Vietnamese War, was emollient and agreeable. I used to spend some time dissuading Maître Blum from taking legal action against the press, where I thought this would merely gain publicity of the sort our own royal family would not like. Our talks were interesting, and she clearly knew a good deal about the history of the abdication.

The worst part was the little tea party which was always provided by an ancient maid when I called on her. For this, her cook made a chocolate cake served on a silver plate, and, by French standards or, indeed, any other, it was dry and disgusting. Maître Blum would not let you get away with less than two large slices. When I left Paris, and she and the general both came to my farewell party, Maître Blum was placed in the hands of Phillip Nelson, a young man who had replaced Howard Davies as the ambassador's private secretary. I told Maître Blum that poor Monsieur Nelson did not get much to eat, and that his main passion was chocolate cake. 'May you be forgiven!' said Phillip in an undertone.

Then there was the Lord Mayor of London. I was in Paris when Air Commodore Sir Peter Vanneck retired after a distinguished career in the RAF some years before. He decided to pay a formal visit there, to Paris, with Foreign Office support. Sir Peter paid great attention to the detail of the visit. 'I shall of course wish to bring my halberdiers with me,' he said. He also brought a retired naval captain, who was his private secretary, and various other ceremonial figures who traditionally surround the Lord Mayor, including the Remembrancer, whose duties I never ascertained, but who wore a curious furry hat.

Peter Vanneck was genial and jolly throughout. His French was not bad; he had a holiday house in the department of Corrèze. This was very near where the Mayor of Paris, Jacques Chirac, lived, and in the department which he represented politically. But apart from this there was nothing in common between the two. Chirac's interests were politics, food and women, perhaps in that order, and he had prodigious energy. Vanneck, on the other hand, was interested mainly in the charities he supported as Lord Mayor and in the robes and regalia which the Lord Mayor of London wore on formal occasions. Unfortunately the suitcase containing his glittering collection of chains, badges, medals and orders got lost en route to Paris, and Vanneck had to take his place at the main formal ceremony in his honour at the Hôtel de Ville unadorned by decorations. The French kept their end up well, with the Paris municipal band rather sportingly playing 'Land of Hope and Glory' as the Lord Mayor and his elderly halberdiers trooped their way into the main assembly room. Both Chirac and Vanneck made suitable speeches full of compliments and references to the strength of Anglo-French relations. There was much small talk, both sides being determinedly affable. I felt later, undiplomatically, that a Jacques Chirac/Ken Livingstone ding-dong would have been much more lively, but in the 1970s London had no elected mayor, and I am sure Chirac was not much interested in the gold and enamel badges and chains of office or the furry hats, or the other traditional and funny uniforms worn by the Vanneck entourage.

Chirac's *chef de cabinet* at the town hall was efficient, cultivated and amusing. He turned the visit into a success, at least to outward appearances. He said Chirac drove him mad by his telephone calls, day and night. 'Of course,' he said, 'I do not answer the telephone at night.' I asked him how he managed to do this. 'I can tell by the special way the telephone rings that it is Chirac at the other end,' he said, 'so I pay no attention to it.'

Gifts were exchanged, more amiable speeches made, and we got through the day somehow. Chirac could not have been a more courteous or attentive host, and both he and his wife and Vanneck and his seemed to get on fairly well. But I am bound to say that the contribution to Anglo-French friendship made by the visit seemed a pretty thin one. Foreigners, and this certainly included the French, could never grasp the concept of a city as large as London having no political or popularly elected mayor, and looked on our own Lord Mayor as a mixture of charity fundraiser and chief of protocol, which indeed he was.

18

Under-Secretary

From Paris, I was posted to London and promoted to Under-Secretary. My exact position was sometimes known as the odds and ends 'Under-Secretary' since I had the following, rather diverse, departments under me: United Nations Department, Information Department, Cultural Relations Department, Library and Records Department, Consular Department, Immigration and Visa Department, Treaty and Nationality Department, and for a short while, the Passport Office – Claims Department, I was also advisor to the Archbishop of Canterbury, Robert Runcie, on whom I would call at Lambeth Palace. He would open the door to me personally. 'Thank God you've come,' he'd say. 'My foreign policy is a shambles.' He introduced me to Terry Waite, his personal secretary, with whom I worked closely.

It sounds a tall order, and at times it was. Some of my departments floated along easily, with the complexity of their business and their expertise of their officers rendering it necessary for their overall boss – me – to be consulted only once in a blue moon. The Claims Department and Treaty and Nationality Department were two in much the same category. The most troublesome and busiest was the Cultural Relations Department, it being in practice paymaster of that admirable institution the British Council, on whose board I sat when the head of the Diplomatic Service could not attend himself. The chairman was Sir Charles (Dick)

Troughton, the ex-chairman of W.H. Smith. It had many branches overseas, staffed mostly by enthusiasts for British culture in all its aspects. Some of its staff were erratic, some eccentric and some rather like the madder sort of English schoolmaster, teaching English in schools in far away places, securing places in British universities for their brightest pupils, and often in my view surpassing in value the work of the embassy. From time to time the British Council outraged the Foreign Office and the press with its seeming taste for the avant-garde. A lasting memory is that of a British Council show put on in Paris by a pair called P. Orridge and his partner, Cosy Fanny Tutti. I forget the plot – if indeed there was one – except that a feature of the evening was a totally naked (male) member of the cast making his way along every row of the audience, his private parts dangling in their faces as he did so. There were many complaints, but the show went on, baffling its audiences, particularly in the developing world. By contrast, British Council-supported English Language schools were immensely popular, and well attended, as were the more conventional theatrical performances. I remember a British Council backed *Titus Andronicus*, playing to a largely Spanish audience in Madrid, most of whom seemed fully conversant with the text in English.

There were periodic and serious rows over money, the British Council receiving its funds from the Foreign Office, which were invariably squeezed by the Treasury. Dick Troughton secured a substantial increase in these funds by working his charm and persuasive powers upon Mrs Thatcher, whose top priorities did not necessarily involve the diffusion of British culture overseas. The Council was also responsible for paying university fees for visiting scholars from abroad, but these were cut off at a stroke after the Tory election victory in 1975, by the then Minister of Education, Sir Keith Joseph, without consulting his Cabinet colleagues or the

Foreign Office. It was a monstrous and ill-thought-out decision, which caused immense ill-will abroad, until we were able to put together a scheme which helped the hardest hit overseas students and those most in need.

The Cultural Relations Department also had the job of negotiating cultural agreements with other countries, mostly Communist ones. The most spectacular of these was probably a pompous document covering educational exchanges with Outer Mongolia. It provided for one Mongolian to study English in Britain for a year, and an English student to study at Ulan Bator for the same period. To celebrate the signature of this solemn accord, the Mongolian Ambassador gave a lunch, the main course being small, spicy and rather tasty Mongolian dumplings. The Mongolian student, an amiable young man, was present. I asked him what his work was in Outer Mongolia. 'I am a hunter,' he replied.

There was much humdrum work, but generally it was satisfying. It took me out of the little world of the Foreign Office and into the wider one of the arts, museums, universities and cultural activities of all kinds. The head of the department was John Morgan, whose languages included French, Spanish, Portuguese, Russian, Korean and (though I cannot be sure) Chinese.

Then there was the Information Department, which was the paymaster of the BBC World Service. Our relations with the latter were generally, but not always, harmonious. The Treasury, as was usual, squeezed the sum of money available, and the World Service responded by cutting or threatening to cut one or more of its vernacular services. In its support, it enlisted a powerful lobby of MPs from both sides of the Houses of Parliament. They made much trouble and, in my view, then and now, over-estimated the value to Britain of the World Service, admirable though many of its programmes were. They had sometimes only the vaguest idea of what the World Service did. Visitors taken round Bush House, where the World Service worked, were invariably impressed by its cramped quarters and frugality. They were shown some of the vernacular services at work, a favourite being the Burmese service, staffed by a number of pretty and graceful Burmese girls with large eyes and enormous smiles. The BBC's postbag from listeners in Burma, even though writing letters to the BBC was illegal in that country, amounted to hundreds of letters a year. No one ever thought of scrapping such services, which cost very little. On the other hand, in countries where press freedom existed, the need for a short-wave language service was not always obvious. I remember an argument I had in Spain later on (when ambassador) with the man who ran the BBC Spanish Language Service. He insisted that it was essential. Spain might any day abandon democracy and revert to a dictatorship, with no free press or broadcasting. I could only reply that in nearly five years spent in Spain under Franco's rule I had never come across a single Spaniard who listened, even briefly, to the BBC's Spanish service. Common sense prevailed, and the service was cut.

Of the other departments I supervised in London, I could say much. The Consular Department, with its responsibility for British subjects travelling or resident overseas, had a wider range of functions, ranging from problems caused by muggings or lost passports, to prisoners in jail (there were well over a hundred of these in my time in Spain), mostly for drug smuggling but sometimes for more serious offences such as murder. Traffic accidents, air crashes, and petty crimes committed by Britons were its business too, and cooperation with the Spanish police needed to be, and was, very close. The honorary consul in Benidorm, a youngish British businessman working in Spain, would call on the Spanish police every morning on his way to work and obtain the names of Britons held there overnight (usually for drunkenness or for behaviour derived from it) with a view

135

to securing their release and repatriation – at their expense. Then there were, of course, the football hooligans, a nightmare to control. One group I remember well. Drunk after the game, which I think their club, possibly Chelsea, lost, they sought their bus for the journey home. The bus broke down in a remote area, and they had to spend the remainder of the night in a modest hotel, which they left without paying the bill. Somehow they got themselves back to Madrid, where they demanded that the consulate general get them home. Trefor Llewelyn, the nice (and rugby-playing) consul general in Madrid, put them in the embassy cinema to fill out the forms needed to obtain an advance of money to pay their return fares.

They were an extremely unpleasant lot. Scarett, one of their leaders, had the word 'Forest' tattooed on his lower lip. To keep them quiet and occupied, Trefor said they could play one of their videos on the embassy's machine. The video they chose was the one recording the explosion of the US space vehicle *Challenger*, its entire crew losing their lives, and the hooligans cheered the moment when it blew up. Only two of the hooligans' families in England produced the money for their return home. To the Spaniards, our hooligans were a disgusting spectacle and did our reputation and image no good at all. When we heard of an English team with plans to visit Spain I would call on the police chief or one of his deputies and ask them to be as tough as they wanted to be. Spanish football supporters could be rough and unruly but never as barbaric and nasty as ours.

I used to dread it in London when the head of the Consular Department visited me. He was invariably the bringer of bad news. I once received a visit from a recently released British prisoner in Ocaña jail (an ancient castle near Toledo), who, I think, had been there on a charge of manslaughter. I asked him how Ocaña had been. It was lovely, he said (compared with British ones, with which he also had some previous acquaintance). Once you got used to the food, the sun shone a lot, and drugs were easy to obtain. There were also a lot of British prisoners on the run in Spain, but an extradition treaty with Spain was signed when I was there and some of the worst absconders ('Manchester Billy' and others in my time, the murderer Kenneth Noye more recently) were arrested in a cooperative movement by the Spanish and British police and now languish on long terms in British jails.

I remained in charge of all these departments (except the political side of the United Nations) during the Falklands War. There were plenty of signs of Argentine menace in the weeks leading up to the invasion, but a general reluctance in the Foreign Office to admit that it was a serious possibility. The sense of shock when it actually occurred was tremendous. The Foreign Office were generally regarded as grossly negligent if not traitorous. The fact was that their attention was at the time (as so often) concentrated on matters of wider importance, such as the Arab–Israeli problem and, of all things, the question of international observers at the forthcoming elections in El Salvador. I was at a conference (I forget the subject) at Peterhouse College, Cambridge, at the time, with a few Foreign Office colleagues and MPs. None of us could believe that war would result over a matter of such little material importance to us, but we were all affected by a sense of shame at the pictures of our small marine contingent on the islands surrendering. Our Foreign Secretary, Peter Carrington, resigned, Francis Pym replacing him, and the military task force started to assemble.

I attended a departmental conference in the office on the war every morning and, at one moment, was almost nominated, I suppose as a Spanish speaker, to be liaison officer with the military force on its way to the Falklands. I remember taking out my winter clothing in case I had to go to sea, but the plan was sensibly scrapped (what in any case would my role have been?) Meanwhile the Falkland Islanders, as British subjects living in an occupied territory, came under the protection of the Consular Department, as for that matter did British subjects, or Anglo-Argentines (there were hundreds of these), living in Argentina, many of whom moved quietly to their second homes in Uruguay until they were certain the war was over. The Information Department also had the job of informing our posts in other countries of the course of events. The Consular Department had the job of broadcasting via the BBC World Service, once weekly, a message of encouragement to the Islanders about deliverance being on the way.

I soon developed a Churchillian tone and terms of phrase until someone suggested that the speech-maker should be Rex Hunt, the Governor of the Falklands, now back in England. He knew the Islanders well, while I knew none. I accordingly gave Rex the next broadcast, to discover the next day what had been done by him. Rex, who in normal times would probably have been an administration officer in a small embassy, had virtually given away the Task Force's battle plan by mentioning its route to Port Stanley over the radio. He was summoned by a furious Number 10 Downing Street the next morning to enquire what he had been trying to do, and there was a great row. I do not think he was asked to repeat his broadcasting activity. He was much seen in London in those days, grinning from ear to ear, posing as champion of the Islanders, in whose support he basked. There was, of course, much relief when the Argentines were defeated, even if Mrs Thatcher's reaction to the recaputure of South Georgia ('Rejoice, rejoice!') was, to me at least, embarrassing. The Argentines, for their part, had acted stupidly, failing (like the Spaniards in relation to Gibraltar) to ingratiate themselves with the inhabitants, and postponing perhaps for years the date when the islands might become closer to them. A local note was struck by Mrs

138

Hunt, our daily lady in the village, whose son worked in the engine room on HMS *Hermes*. She wrote on her front window, in Christmas silver spray, 'The Argy navy's got no gravy. Up yours, Galtiary [*sic*].' Meanwhile, there was another local note when Alfredo Astiz, who was personally responsible for the disappearance of many anti-Galtieri activists by pushing them out of aeroplanes, or otherwise arranging their murder, was captured in South Georgia and imprisoned, while the war lasted, in the Royal Military Police Barracks in Chichester, near where we lived.

19

Madrid (First Time Round)

In 1966 I was posted from London to Madrid as head of chancery. As we crossed the border from France into San Sebastián, we were immediately struck by the run-down appearance of the buildings and comparative poverty of the people, as well as a certain old-fashioned air. The latter was most evident in San Sebastián in the Basque Country, where well-dressed nannies wheeled their prams along the pretty seashore. We then spent two days driving to Madrid, through the Basque Country and via Burgos over the dry Castilian plain, over the Guadarrama Mountains to the awful hotel selected for us by the unimaginative administration officer, who a few days later found a service flat where we lived more or less comfortably for a while before finding a house.

The house we eventually found was just a short walk from Franco's Park, a vast expanse of scrub full of game and home to the Zarzuela Palace (where Juan Carlos, known then as the 'Prince of Spain', lived with his small family). Our house was owned by a kindly but ancient Basque *marquesa*, whom after a while we persuaded to dig a deep well for us, the existing water supply being unreliable. I used to talk from time to time to the well-diggers, far below me at the bottom of the very deep hole they had dug. It was the time of the 1966 World Cup in Britain, which we narrowly won. The well-diggers were quite confident that we would do so. I said there could be no certainty over this. The well-diggers were quite sure of this on the grounds that we would be playing at home. I said there was no questioning the referee's decisions.

'Oh yes, there is!' shouted one well-digger from the bottom of his deep pit. 'Particularly if you pay him enough!'

The Franco dictatorship could be stern and cruel. There was a parliament of a kind (the Cortes), but no political parties were allowed – as a member of the Cortes, you represented a social group. It was what I believe is known as a corporate state. Families, businessmen and others were not elected directly and freely by popular vote, but nominated by the National Movement, a bogus sort of assembly, formed by a fusion between the Falange and like-minded groupings who supported Franco in the Civil War. Members wore smart white jackets on formal occasions and did the Nazi salute. The Cortes had no serious powers of its own, its main function being a rubber stamp for legislation (much of it illiberal) put before them by Franco or his ministers. Franco's regime, especially in his advancing years, had no coherent ideology, no feeling for democracy as we understand it, and was extremely hard on anyone who opposed it publicly. There was no free press, although skilful editors often found their way around the system of self-censorship.

If you kept your head down, the dictatorship did not particularly bother anyone much. The growing middle class were, on the whole, left free to start businesses and to make money from them. Mary and I noticed that none of our Spanish friends ever seemed to complain about taxation. We concluded that not all of them paid tax at any serious level. For them, life was good. Domestic service was scarce but by no means impossible. They lived well.

At first we found it difficult to get to know Spaniards. Then it dawned on us that much of their talk concerned their own families, often closely related. Once you knew the families, or even some of them, you admitted yourself to an exclusive closed circle. Then there was the question of Gibraltar, of which more below. My constant contact with the Spanish foreign ministry over Gibraltar made it possible to gain many new Spanish friends, who were agreeable and friendly, no matter how fierce the arguments we might have had over the Rock. The hardliners in the foreign ministry were doing no more than reflect the obsessive views of Fernando Maria Castiella, the Foreign Minister. His office was lined with prints, some of them very good, of Gibraltar and other topics got so little attention that his ministry was sometimes known as the 'Ministry of the Foreign Affair'. None of this affected the friendship towards us of the ministry personnel, even though the latter were loyal servants of their government. A major exception was Jesus Ezquerra, the uncouth under-secretary for Europe, including Gibraltar. He was rough and rude. Someone should have told him that was not the way to deal with the British. He left Madrid before I did to become Ambassador to the Holy See, where he vanished from my life. I think he had a row with a cardinal, which shortened his tour in Rome. The US Ambassador, who had been under-secretary in the State Department during the Falklands War, was a generally courteous but malign influence and not to be trusted – by me at any rate. He was disliked in Spain, largely for his arrogance.

Gibraltar dominated my first spell in Spain in the 1960s. The Spaniards never understood that all that mattered to us was that the Gibraltarians should be free to choose between Britain and Spain, independence being ruled out by the colony's founding document, the Treaty of Utrecht of 1714. The Spaniards rejected any form of hearts-and-minds campaign designed to ingratiate themselves with the Gibraltarians, whom on the whole they despised, pursuing instead a hostile and legalistic approach that alienated precisely the people they should have befriended. This meant closing the border

142

and making life very difficult for everyone involved. For our part, over three centuries we had often done things which were patronising or downright illegal, compounding the Gibraltarians' dislike of Spaniards and vice versa. We had also devised a constitution for Gibraltarians which was effectively set in concrete, making it impossible for us to change anything except sacking the chief minister (something you cannot do more than once in a blue moon), in my time the popular and broad-minded Sir Joshua Hassan. Later on the embassy and Foreign Office spent months devising an agreement providing for an airport for joint use by Britain and Spain, which the Gibraltarians rejected as they saw it as another move on our part to move Gibraltar closer to Spain. Meanwhile I made occasional 'liaison' visits to the Rock to talk to the governor, Admiral Sir Varyl Begg, whom my boss in Madrid, Sir John Russell, used to refer to impolitely as 'f****** old Teakface'.

I met Sir Joshua Hassan's two successors during my first spell at Madrid. The first, Major Peliza (of the Gibraltar Regiment), proved difficult to find. I only tracked him down late one night on a rare visit to the Rock with the assistance of the ADC to the governor. He was in a small Gibraltarian restaurant, effusive, cheerful but considerably the worse for wear, and wholly incoherent as a result and distinctly unsteady on his feet. His successor, Joe Bassano, would in Britain have been a lower middle-ranking trade-union leader, who had the same rapport with the ordinary voter, but whose understanding stopped there. He was anti-Spanish and anti-British and with no presence or charisma. When I first called on him I mistook him for the electrician who had come to repair the lights in his office. Gibraltar was and still is a little free port of small importance to Britain ruled by little men whose self-importance seemed to me their chief characteristic.

Earlier on, Fernando Olivié, the Spanish under-secretary

143

for Europe, published a huge book detailing every instance of the rightness of Spain's claim over the Rock (including press cuttings and anything else that favoured the Spanish case – Nicko Henderson, the number two in Madrid at the time referred to it as 'Fernando's Bumper Christmas Annual'). It had no influence on anyone – elsewhere in Spain no one, apart from dedicated *franquistas*, seemed to care about it much. In the Basque Country I once mentioned Gibraltar as a contentious issue between us. 'Where?' they asked. In Cataluña the reaction was the same. 'Let's talk about something that matters' was the reaction of the local government there.

The problem will not be sorted out for a generation or two, assuming the use of common sense by the three parties involved. Meanwhile Her Majesty's ambassador in Madrid will waste much time on it and his irritation will grow. In Franco's time, nearly all the daily papers carried an offensive article on the front page about Britain and Gibraltar. I translated these, and it did my Spanish no end of good.

The other question of great concern for us was what would happen when Franco died (he lived until 1975). The young generation – apolitical in general – cared little. The middle aged and old told me that the Spaniards, with their passionate natures and tendency for violence, needed very strong government, if something like a new civil war was to be avoided. There was in the event no violence, Spaniards of all sorts proving docile and the growing middle class too preoccupied with making money. A peaceful transition to democracy was achieved under a wise and prudent king, with the supportive Socialist Party running his government, and an Opposition party of generally moderate views making much noise but taking little action. The trade unions caused much of the trouble. It was satisfactory to see not only a modern Spain joining other European democracies under able leadership, but also conventional wisdom confounded on such a decisive scale. Long may this last, and long may Spain prosper!

Meanwhile the Civil War had receded, not wholly but far more quickly than I would have thought possible, despite the appalling savagery and cruelties on both sides. Most of our friends, to the extent that they were political, were middle to right wing, but there were plenty of people from the left. Some of these, who had overstepped the government's accepted lines of tolerance, were exiled for a while to remote rural villages. Viewed at first as dangerous 'Reds', they generally settled in, and I heard of at least two who, when their exile ended, were given send-off parties by the village which housed them, including in one case the priest who had preached a sermon against him on his arrival.

When I arrived in Madrid for the second time in 1984, as ambassador, one of the first things I did was to visit, as an ordinary member of the public, the handsome El Pardo Palace, where Franco lived after the Civil War. The guide in charge of groups of tourists treated it as if it had been any old palace once inhabited by a figure from history. He pointed out the generalissimo's office, his bedroom and so on with a monotone voice bereft of emotion. It was as though we were being shown round a rather old-fashioned museum that had nothing to do with the turbulent years of Spain's recent history.

20

Spain and People In It

Mary and I were in Spain from 1966 to 1971, when I was the head of chancery. We were in the country again from 1984 to 1990 when I was ambassador. During our first period in Spain Franco was still in power; by the second period Spain was a democratic monarchy ruled by King Juan Carlos.

This is not the place to write an essay on Spain. It is a richly complex country with a dazzling history, and after spending about ten years there I could not write about it without risking my account being long and biased. Instead, I thought it best to single out a few people whom I knew well and who influenced my time and life there.

That means starting at the top, with the King. Mary and I had both known the King and Queen in the 1960s when he was living very much under the shadow of Franco. Franco's hope seemed to be that Juan Carlos would succeed him when he died, and carry on his half-baked semi-fascist policies, with absolutely no question of reconciliation with the Republican enemies whom he had defeated in the Civil War. In the earlier days (the sixties) the King lived a fairly quiet life not far from Franco's own palace, and kept his relations with him on an even keel. He would see Franco fairly frequently but, I am told, rarely discussed serious matters with him. Indeed, most people, even his oldest military acquaintances, like Admiral Nieto Antunez, a friend of many years and fishing companion, found conversation with Franco far from easy. The King, for his part, was always dignified but also jolly and cheerful, and had a lot of fun. If he wanted something from you, he would buttonhole you at a ceremony or get hold of you by whatever means he could, by telephone if necessary, and talk frankly in whatever language came easiest to him at the time. He was a member of the Spanish Olympic sailing team, through merit not rank, and like many of his compatriots was a very good shot of game of all kinds.

The Spaniards had a certain disdain for the institution of monarchy, but they liked the King as a person for his warm and friendly approach, a characteristic which the Bourbon royal monarchs seem to have displayed consistently since the days they came to power, however foolish or incompetent they may have been politically. They liked the Queen, too, for her dignity, her cultural interests (especially music) and her ability to smile. The King and Queen had a lot of friends, but both of them saw to it that most of them were generally never too close nor too intimate, thus avoiding the mistake made by the King's grandfather, Alfonso XIII, who built up a large court around him which had a tendency to develop into a centre of jealousy and intrigue. The King and Queen's court hardly existed at all, consisting of a small group of officers and ladies whom they trusted and who trusted them. Once, when a group of Spanish ladies were having tea with the Queen, they talked of her burden of work and thought it was time she appointed a lady-in-waiting. The Queen said politely that she did not need a lady-in-waiting, but if any of her friends knew of a good and reliable personal maid she would be glad to take her on. There was no more talk of ladies-in-waiting thereafter.

Then there was Don Juan, the Count of Barcelona, the King's father, who had fallen out over the years with Franco and only occasionally visited Spain privately when Franco was alive. He was a great Anglophile, having served as a lieutenant in a number of ships in the Royal Navy between the wars and was a friendly old gentleman with pronounced festive tendencies despite his great age. The last time I saw him, not long before he died, I learned he was shortly to visit London (where he would usually stay with his friend the Queen Mother). When I asked him what the purpose of his visit was on this occasion, he asked for a pencil and paper (his vocal chords had been much affected by cancer) and wrote on it 'To have a binge'.

A little later, thanks largely to the persistence of my naval attaché, I received a telegram from Buckingham Palace asking me to find out if the rank of honorary admiral in the Royal Navy would be acceptable to Don Juan. Antonio, my driver, and I, after a long day driving in the car, eventually tracked down Don Juan at the Spanish naval base at Cartagena where he was living frugally on his small and rather elderly (British-made) yacht called the *Giralda*. When I told him of the purpose of my mission he was silent for a while, but then his eyes misted up. He summoned his ADC and pointed silently to a shelf in his cabin where there was a bottle of whisky. We drank this. While we did so he composed a longish letter of gratitude to the Queen, which I promised to send off on my return to Madrid later in the day. When I left the yacht after more whisky and conversation, Don Juan whispered hoarsely, 'Phew, what a relief. When they told me that the British ambassador wanted to see me, immediately I thought to myself "My God, what have I done?"' He swore himself to secrecy until an announcement about his honorary appointment was made, but when I eventually returned to Madrid that evening I bumped into a relation of his by marriage who said, 'A great thing you did for Don Juan today, Nicky; it has given him immense pleasure.' I learnt later that this leak probably came from the King himself, whom his father had told of my visit and its purpose shortly after I left.

Geoffrey Howe and the author in the garden of the British Residence in Madrid during the Madrid Summit, June 1989.

Painting on board the Royal Yacht Britannia as a guest of Queen Elizabeth the Queen Mother on a private trip to the West Country, Summer 1997.

The author with his brother Charles in the library at Goodwood.

The author's grandchildren wearing some of the author's hats. Freddie, Rufus and Thomas Caldecott in the garden of South Nore 1998.

A gathering of the family after a cricket match at Goodwood in the Summer of 2001.

Lettice, Lucy and Harry Cornell, 2002.

The Spanish Ambassador to London, José Joaquín Puig de la Bellacasa, and his wife Paz, photographed at the time of the visit of the King and Queen of Spain to London in April 1986. José Joaquín and Paz were close friends of the author and Mary.

Painting at the kitchen table at South Nore. The author with his grandchildren Alice and Arthur Lindsell, 2001.

La Cartuja, Val de Mossa, Mallorca - watercolour by the author.

Some weeks later we had a small celebration to mark this event on one of Her Majesty's ships, with our own chief of naval staff present. There was a luncheon on board, and speeches, and aerobatic demonstrations by helicopters. There were also many toasts. I had arranged for some of Don Juan's closest friends to be present. One was the Duke of Alburquerque, Spain's most distinguished amateur jockey and horseman who had ridden several times in the Grand National. He had completed the race on several occasions but had never been placed. He was so full of metal objects following his falls from horses that the security devices through which he had to walk at airports practically exploded when he did so. He was a wonderful horseman and a brave and efficient soldier and a good friend to Mary and me. Many of the crew on our Royal Navy vessel had heard of him and his bravery as a horseman, and he was happy to receive their recognition. He was a devoted monarchist, with a lineage stretching back for centuries, and a man of impeccable manners.

Then there was another great friend of the 1960s called Fernando Moran, a diplomat who was at that time in the relatively obscure job of Director General for African Affairs, but who more importantly was also a senior member of the Spanish Socialist Party. He was a thoughtful and broadminded Asturian, a convinced Socialist and a popular figure in public life even if the popularity sometimes deteriorated into ridicule. Fernando always had time to see me, but his working methods were chaotic. He chain-smoked, and when I went to see him at the Spanish foreign ministry his smoking sometimes severely reduced the visibility in his office. We also had a whisky or two. When I left Madrid in 1971 he had been posted to London as consul in the Spanish Embassy there, with what appeared to be routine duties. But he was always an influential figure in the Spanish Socialist Party and had a sharp understanding of politics in his own country

149

and elsewhere. I remember being with him and watching a British general election from our house in London and noting how quickly he grasped the sometimes mysterious processes of our own political system. When I returned to Spain as ambassador in 1984 three principals involved in the presentation of my credentials – the King, Fernando and myself – were all friends and on Christian name terms, a rarity on these occasions.

It was Fernando who introduced me to another friend, Enrique Tierno Galvan, an elderly Socialist also and a figure of great prestige, who by the time of my second tour in Madrid was its mayor, and as such both popular and respected. He was widely known as 'El Viejo Professor', or the Old Professor. He died when I was in Madrid as ambassador and was widely mourned by the populace for his idiosyncratic ways and good sense of humour. He used to write homilies in the newspapers urging the *madrileños* to be more careful over such things as dropping rubbish in the streets, and not to abandon their pets when they went off for their seaside summer holidays.

As important as anyone I knew was José Joaquin Puig de la Bellacasa, whose time as ambassador in London coincided very closely with my own in Madrid. We both saw the need for much closer relations between Britain and Spain in the context of the European Union, NATO, and mutual exchanges of trade between the two countries. What we both regarded as ludicrous were the attitudes of both sides towards Gibraltar (or rather, in our case I would say our parliamentary attitude rather than the governmental one) and more particularly that of the Gibraltarians themselves. Anglo-Spanish relations, especially cultural ones, were very strong, largely due to the manic interest and indefatigable energy of Stewart Smith, a star who was the head of the British Council in Spain, with whom I worked closely and harmoniously in different parts of the country. We opened several successful British Institutes, including English language schools, in such places as Segovia and Jaen, both small towns where the institutes were immensely popular and well attended.

British and Spanish interests in many other parts of the world coincided where they were not identical. Literary and academic links were strong, and ordinary people in both countries on the whole liked and respected each other (the exception of course being football hooligans, generally regarded as a purely British phenomenon). It was only the intractable problem of Gibraltar which frustrated the efforts of both sides trying to improve the overall relationship to our mutual benefit. Puig and I were frank about our own people, seeking with some success to keep our worst ministers out of Spain and theirs out of Britain. We largely succeeded in this.

Another extremely valuable friend was José Maria Areilza, the Count of Motrico, whom I had come to know well, with his family, when he was Spanish ambassador in Washington in the late 1950s during my first posting there. When I arrived in Madrid as ambassador he was the first person to telephone me with a message of welcome. I asked if he would one day brief me on the state of affairs in Spain. 'I'll come and see you right away,' he said and was with me in about half an hour, staying to give me a richly amusing account of the Spanish political, social and even sexual scandals of the day. His experience was immensely wide. He had started off as a young enthusiast for the right and became the Mayor of Bilbao (he was a Basque) at an earlier age than any of his predecessors. His main and abiding loyalty was to the Spanish royal family and, in particular, to Don Juan, the King's father. By the time we met again in Madrid he had been ambassador in Washington and held many other influential jobs. He had written in his early days a book attacking the British position in Gibraltar in vigorous

151

terms and was generally regarded as a rather erratic Conservative of good standing.

Now in the 1980s, he had shifted to the left of the political spectrum, and, with his knowledge of the outside world and experience of public affairs, was very much a figure to reckon with in Spain, particularly amongst the monarchists. I remember him once being put under a form of house arrest by Franco's government for something he had said or done which gave offence to the regime. His immediate reaction was to give a large party for all his friends. He called it his 'come if you dare' party. It was strictly speaking an illegal gathering under Franco's laws, but I believe there were only a few people who did not turn up at it. He was a subtle, clever and intellectually agile person, not always universally trusted, but always arousing respect, and always amusing and indiscreet.

The Prince and Princess of Wales visited Madrid officially in 1986. It was not a happy occasion. They both knew the Spanish royal family quite well, through mutual friends and having spent brief holidays with them in Mallorca. But it was clear that their marriage was already in trouble. They stayed at the El Pardo Palace, which had been Franco's home in Madrid, and was now the Royal guest house, an elegant seventeenth to eighteenth-century chateau a few miles outside the city. They had brought with them a number of – two dozen or so – journalists. In innocence we all hoped they would report on royal visits to places of spectacular beauty such as Toledo and Salamanca. Not at all. Press interest seemed confined to discovering whether the Prince and Princess shared the same bedroom, and of course the same bed. The Waleses hosted a reception for the journalists at El Pardo in the hope of establishing an atmosphere of friendly informality. It didn't. The reception was a flop, and it was, I understand, an experiment which was not attempted again.

152

The journalists (the photographers in particular) squabbled endlessly, and disagreeably, and in seeking the best vantage point, one trod on Mary's foot in Salamanca, nearly breaking her toe, and preventing her wearing her shoes at the dinner-dance we gave for about 150 people that evening. It poured with rain the whole time; fortunately the marquee imported from Barcelona and erected by an efficient Catalan firm proved stable and waterproof. The two Spanish infantas (Princesses) came, and I think had a nice time. Don Juan seemed to much enjoy dancing with Princess Diana. Terry Venables came from Barcelona, where he was successfully managing the football club and had become a national Catalan hero, and was his chirpy self. We gave our guests an English dinner, ending with Queen of Puddings, which was much praised by our Spanish guests, although the Prince of Wales thought it a curious choice. The next day the King (at the wheel) drove his royal guests to Toledo, about an hour away. On their walk through the narrow streets of the ancient city, the Prince of Wales bought a handsome ceramic object, for which his ADC paid. The King, later on, told me how amazed he was that the Prince carried no money himself. 'How can you get to know the people,' he asked me, 'if you never carry any cash with you?' I have to say that the Princess of Wales was not very happy in Spain. Her personal problems aside, she was soon bored with the cathedrals and galleries, of which Spain has quite a few. She was unfailingly polite, if rather remote throughout. I think one of the things she enjoyed the most was when the helicopter in which she left Toledo drenched most of the reporters and photographers watching her departure with rainwater. She cheered loudly.

Nowadays, ministers from all countries are always on the move visiting each other. When I was in Spain I think almost every one of our Cabinet ministers came there at one time or another. We had two visits from Mrs Thatcher when she was Prime Minister. The first was the only time a British prime minister had ever visited Spain officially. It was a bilateral visit in that it involved Britain and Spain and no other country. She arrived with her husband, Denis, and her close team of familiars – Charles Powell and Bernard Ingham. The idea was to discuss matters of common concern, Gibraltar and the European Community being, of course, high on the list of contentious issues.

She arrived late one evening having flown from Bruges, where the previous day she had made the now celebrated speech defining Britain's attitude at the time (or hers at any rate) to the European Community. We had supper, and afterwards I briefed her on the next day's programme. To my consternation she yawned and her eyes began to close. She was obviously very tired. I raised my eyebrows at Charles Powell, her private secretary, and he whispered, 'Don't worry, she will be perfectly OK in the morning.' She was. It is true that she only needed a few hours' sleep at night.

The next day I took her on the sort of visit which prime ministers do on these occasions. She went to see the King and had a long session with Prime Minister Felipe González, with whom she had a vigorous argument about Gibraltar, not always getting her facts right. My Spanish opposite number in London and I sat in on the meeting as uneasy spectators, both wishing that the two principals could find more to agree upon. Then there was a luncheon hosted by the Spanish Prime Minister. I suppose about 30 of us were seated on separate round tables. Mrs Thatcher sat next to the Spanish Prime Minister on one side, but they had no common language. I sat a little further down, next to the Prime Minister's wife, a pretty lady who was a secondary school teacher. One of the ambassador's roles on these occasions is to keep the conversational ball rolling, and Señora de González talked to me about her teaching, saying that she was having a rest for one year to give greater support to her husband. I said: 'Mrs González is a secondary school teacher but is having a rest for one year to give her time to help with her husband's duties.' Mrs Thatcher reacted strongly to this, her eyes blazing. 'Rest!' she said, 'Rest! You tell Mrs González from me that I have been an MP now for over 25 years and *I* don't need a rest!' As so often, I found myself having to turn the words around in Spanish so they sounded at least polite. In the end, Mrs Thatcher and Mr González both made friendly and agreeable speeches and the luncheon broke up. The lunch had been produced by Arzak, Spain's foremost chef with an international reputation, and owner of a wonderful restaurant in the Basque Country (I think he had three Michelin stars). There was a man with a chef's hat on hanging around so I said to him, 'Will you please tell Señor Arzak what a delicious lunch he laid on for Mrs Thatcher and how much we all appreciated it.' The man in the chef's hat said simply, 'I am Arzak,' leaving me with the need to find a reply to cover my embarrassment.

On our way to see the Spanish Prime Minister before lunch, I said to Mrs Thatcher, 'The Prime Minister is, as you know, also head of the Spanish Socialist Party, but he is very much not the sort of Socialist you and I know, more of a Social Democrat. Mrs Thatcher said, 'Don't tell me that,' adding, 'I know all these people, they are all the same.'

Then I took her to the Spanish Cortes, or Parliament, where there was a meeting with leaders of the political parties. It threw up few points of interest until she came to Nicolas Sartorius, a member of an old and distinguished Spanish family. Nicolas made some remarks which revealed his sympathies; although relatively young, and an aristocrat, he had for some time been head of the Spanish Communist Party. 'I have heard all this from the Soviet leadership,'

155

said Mrs Thatcher, with a touch of acidity. It was clear that the other party leaders appreciated her point of view as she got a standing ovation when she left, which cheered her up a lot. She was very happy to have been so well received and applauded. On the way back to her car, discreetly parked not too far away, she met a 'spontaneously' assembled group of Spanish boys and girls from the excellent British Council school and she chatted to them briefly. She also received greetings from elderly spectators or passers-by, the sort who sat on park benches with cigarettes dangling from their lower lip, either reading tabloid newspapers or just sitting. I don't think she understood what they were saying. Their line was mostly that Spain needed a strong leader, like her, like Franco. She liked that too.

The last meeting I organised for her was about a dozen people, mostly Spanish businessmen with views on economic and financial matters or captains of Spanish industry. I agreed with Charles Powell that we would have general conversation before lunch, until the start of the first course when I would ask one of the Spanish guests to embark on a theme in which Mrs Thatcher would like to join, and which with luck would provoke a discussion. I therefore got hold of Miguel Boyer, the ex-Minister for Economics, and he readily agreed to kick off a discussion of this kind at the appropriate time. Unfortunately, he chose as his theme Third World debt with particular reference to South America, a subject for which Mrs Thatcher had contempt and certainly no interest whatsoever. When, after much too long, Boyer had finished speaking, there was a silence and Mrs Thatcher said, 'So what?' It was an awkward and chilling moment, and another challenge for the ambassador's conversational persiflage, but happily one of my other guests then seized the initiative and started off on another topic in which Mrs Thatcher did display an interest.

For some reason Mrs Thatcher did not seem to like being

156

out of doors. Mary tried to persuade her that it would be nice to have dinner in the garden or, later, to be photographed there with the embassy domestic staff. She seemed to resist this and we wondered why. She was evidently one of those people who preferred to operate in a confined space. Denis Thatcher, a very nice man, was magnificent in his support of her. Mary took him on and did some sightseeing with him, fuelling him from time to time with gin and tonics ('No ice in it, please, dear'). He was polite and accommodating at all times, but I do not think he much appreciated Picasso's *Guernica*, which had become a symbol for Republicans in the Civil War, and which we took him to see as one of the sights of Madrid. He muttered that this was not really his style, and I am sure he meant what he said. Although always a courteous guest, Mrs Thatcher was not strong on small talk, and in two days she never asked Mary a single question about Spain and her life in it. She was focused, and the focus was not on politics in Spain, but mostly in England. When she finally left, by air, she thanked me and said, 'Your Mr González is a very impressive person.' It was nice to hear that opinion, but the 'your' made it sound just a little bit as if I was in Spanish pay, not hers. She wrote me a very polite and complimentary letter afterwards.

Mrs Thatcher's second visit was vastly more dramatic. It was to attend a summit of the European heads of government, with the European financial system on the agenda. She stayed not with us but with all European prime ministerial colleagues at the Ritz Hotel, her detective making a big, and to me, wholly unnecessary fuss about security. When she arrived at the airport for the summit meeting she was accompanied by the Foreign Secretary, Sir Geoffrey Howe, and a small platoon of senior servants. Mary and I greeted her at the foot of the steps of the aircraft, and as we walked towards the VIP lounge, Mary whispered to me, 'There is something not quite right here – what is it?' Women,

157

especially Mary, are often more perceptive than men on these occasions, and all was indeed not right. The main thing was that Mrs Thatcher and Geoffrey Howe were not on speaking terms, he and Nigel Lawson, the Chancellor of the Exchequer, having threatened to resign from their offices the day before in London, unless Mrs Thatcher subscribed to wording about the European Monetary System proposed by the two.

It was a lovely evening, and we had a dinner planned in our garden. In the car I said that I hoped Mrs Thatcher would come to it. To my surprise, she declined, saying she had so much work to do with Charles Powell that she really must spend the evening hours alone working with him. I, of course, fell in with this, but feared that our dinner party might well collapse without her. I approached Geoffrey Howe and said I imagined if Mrs Thatcher couldn't come to dinner because of her work, the same applied to him. He replied robustly that he had every intention of dining with us, as did his staff. It then finally dawned on me that the row over his threatened resignation the day before had seriously affected their relationship. In the meetings that followed, she managed either to ignore him or put him down in a way that must have hurt him and caused him much offence and had much to do with his resignation a little later, and the now famous speech which accompanied it.

The atmosphere was not a happy one. The Prime Minister's party and Sir Geoffrey Howe's spent much time muttering to me about the monstrous and disloyal behaviour of the other. I sat in at most of the meetings, mostly with my mouth shut, as did nearly everyone else. The person who it seemed to me could really handle Mrs Thatcher was Sir David (now Lord) Hannay, who was the head of our delegation to the European Community in Brussels and a clever person, sharp and quick and at all times a clear and firm advocate, not afraid to tell his Prime Minister firmly when he thought her wrong. And of course Bernard Ingham, her spokesman, with whom some time earlier I had to share a double bed in a crowded Washington Hotel. It is worth a short word about this. It was in the closing days of Ted Heath's government, when Bernard Ingham and I were in Washington for a conference on European energy with our respective bosses, Alec and Peter Carrington. There had been a mix-up over our hotel room, and there was only one booked for Bernard and me in the Hay-Adams Hotel, after a long and exhausting day. Fortunately, the bed was a very large one. I slept one side, and Bernard the other. It wasn't a bad night, all things being considered, and Bernard and I were in good form the next morning. Bernard did not allude to this incident in his own memoirs, I think, because he felt readers might have misunderstood him.

When Mrs Thatcher was staying with us she was out at meetings much of the time, leaving Mary in the house with the friendly and charming Mrs Crawford ('Crawfie'). She was Mrs Thatcher's constant companion, and personal adviser on all sorts of things, especially clothes (Aquascutum featured prominently). 'What shall I put her in today?' Crawfie would ask. Crawfie was cooperative and made the visit a much more relaxed occasion than it might have been. We also became aware that, however tough Mrs Thatcher was with her own senior advisers and antagonists, she was always gentle and kind with her own entourage, however junior their rank.

In a fairly short space of time, Mary and I made it our business to travel as much and as often as possible, and I believe we have been to more places in Spain than almost any Spaniard we know. One particularly memorable visit was to Granada, that beautiful but tourist-filled city. A lot of British tourists were getting mugged or robbed in Granada, and the British press was making a great fuss about this. I though it might be a general help if I made a special visit there in the company of a few British journalists to find out what the facts were, and to warn tourists to be sensible and on their guard. I had a good meeting with the local police, and the usual excellent lunch, when I got a message from the Mayor of Granada, saying he would like to see me right away. I made my way to his handsome eighteenth-century town hall, which appeared to be entirely empty.

Eventually I found his secretary, who said that the mayor was most anxious to see me in his main patio, where he was sitting in judgement. I duly found the mayor sitting in a red plush chair in the handsome central courtyard of the town hall, behind a long table. On the other side of the table there were 20 or so men in suits, some of them shifty-looking, and all exhibiting signs of anxiety. The mayor indicated a seat beside him, and I asked him what on earth was going on. Perhaps, I thought, this was some sort of ancient court where petty criminals were examined before being put on trial. 'No, no,' said the mayor, and it was clear I was not about to learn something new about the Spanish judicial system. 'The fellows you see on the other side of the table,' said the Mayor, 'are Granada's most distinguished bartenders and I am judging the "Grenada Cocktail of the Year" competition. Try this one,' and I duly took a good swallow of the front-running candidate in the cocktail competition. While grateful for my admittance to this solemn ceremony and wiping my streaming eyes, I resolved to leave the cocktail circuit alone when I was next in those parts.

Social life, or rather diplomatic/social life was exhausting and intense. Two distinguished visitors in our time were Gilbert and George, the well-known painters (mostly of young men) on a huge scale. They were imaginative and technically proficient, their subjects intended to shock.

160

Thousands saw their week-long show. We gave a party for them, and found them agreeable and polite, dressed in pinstripe suits. Mary and I attended their opening night and posed in front of one of the largest. This had the word 'shit' in huge letters on the canvas and we hoped it would be reproduced in the British press. Unfortunately the latter found something more interesting and shocking. Gilbert and George came with a large entourage, including a beautiful young man who turned out to be valet-cum-fixer to the two. I asked him what he did and he said, 'Man, I kinda look after the two of them.' I think the two would have been lost without him.

It was extraordinary to see how well known the two were in Spain and how popular they were among people of all ages. I think more Spaniards knew about them than their English or Italian (Gilbert was Italian) compatriots.

During our first spell in Madrid, our driver was Luis Gomez, a young man in his twenties, amiable, but unreliable. One day there was a referendum to rubber stamp Franco's 'Organic Law', which, I suppose, was meant to confirm the constitution he had devised for the future. You had to vote or risk a fine. Luis was a registered voter in Toledo, where his father had a smallholding. Remembering too late to warn me, Luis 'borrowed' my car just in time to get to Toledo before the polling booths shut and he avoided his fine. I awaited his return with mounting rage. When he eventually did return it was with a dead baby lamb slung across his shoulders, looking for all the world like a shepherd in an illustration from what Charles and I as small children used to call a 'Jesus Book'.

Luis got away, too, with his Christmas present to the family – a turkey – again from his family smallholding. He presented us with this proudly. It was, however, still alive, highly active and flapping around in the car. Our small domestic staff became hysterical, and as Mary and I had never slain a turkey before we were also nonplussed. Not for the first time, our children's Nanny came to the rescue – seizing the turkey by the legs, she spooned a generous dose of Spanish brandy down its gullet. The turkey sprawled limply on the floor, and Nanny finished it off, by strangulation or throat-cutting, I forget which.

But easily Luis' most spectacular act was setting fire to our house an hour or so before we held a very large cocktail party there for over a hundred people. He had been told to turn on the lights in the garden, a task which he accomplished with an unexpected but complete degree of success, producing not just light but flames. Once Mary had got him to the nearest hospital to treat the severe burns which affected his hands there remained the question of the main fire, blazing merrily on one side of the house. Fortunately, our landlord and next-door neighbour, who was also a friend of ours, owned several cinemas in Madrid and he had a small squad of electricians and firemen on permanent standby. They arrived promptly and put out the fire but could not restore the electricity. The party therefore took place by candlelight which our guests thought imaginative and romantic ('How charming,' people said). Once again, Luis got away with it. But when I returned as ambassador ten or so years later, we did not re-employ him. By then he had in any case turned himself into a waiter for hire, which no doubt made him more money, and he looked very elegant in his white waiter's coat, handing round the drinks. He also drove part-time for my friend Stewart Smith, the head of the British Council, who described him with fair accuracy as 'not a great human being'.

Luis was not a brave man. He once had an argument with Juan, the housekeeper and odd-job man in the first home we rented in Madrid. He and Juan fell out over some trivial matter and decided to settle the matter with their fists. They peeled off their coats and squared up to each other, looking like old-fashioned bare-knuckled fighters. I cannot remember either landing a punch. I happened to be in bed next door with flu and shouted at them both to stop. They took no notice, but when I entered the sitting room and shouted again to them to clear off they both slunk away. Neither was hurt, and the quarrel (whatever it was about) was not continued. Perhaps it was a domestic row about money, food or cleaning, or perhaps one had insulted the other's mother. I did not pursue this, nor did they.

The Hubble telescope is the most modern and possibly the largest in the world. It was built on the Island of La Palma, the most isolated of the Canary Islands, with no beaches, and few tourists – making it ideal for observing the night skies and the usually cloudless day sky. There was considerable interest among astronomers in the UK and elsewhere, and the King decided to make an important occasion of the opening. Virtually every European head of state came and many important politicians. The King was rather annoyed that the Prince of Wales, whose programme had been fixed for months ahead, could not come, and telephoned me when I was about to go to lunch one day. Could we not provide someone more senior than the Duke of Gloucester, whom he personally liked, but who would be outranked by most of the other guests?

Eventually the King acquiesced and was on his jolliest form as we wound our dangerous way round the unpaved road up to the summit. The King spent a long time pushing the wheel-chaired Lady Manton around and mixing with everyone present. He turned the occasion into the happiest of parties, as he so often did.

Among those present at the telescope opening was the eccentric but amusing artist, sculptor and architect called Cesar Manrique, who was responsible for much of the architecture and construction of the telescope installation on

163

the island of La Palma and other Canary Islands. He had designed and built his own house on the island of Fuerteventura where he took advantage of the soft volcanic rock to build it underground so as to keep the climate, the wind and the sand at bay. For the telescope he designed new, imaginative and colourful flags for each country represented, which lined the perilous road to the summit of La Palma and were much admired. He was lively, amusing and apparently ageless.

Robert Maxwell telephoned me one day in Madrid from the Ritz Hotel where he was staying. He was attempting, as far as I could understand, to set up a television deal with the all-powerful Polanco Media Group, headed by Jesus Polanco, who was one of the most powerful men in Spain at the time. He was known informally as 'Jesus del Gran Poder', meaning 'Jesus of the Great Power', after one of the immense floats carried in procession through Seville in Holy Week, accompanied by cowled supporters, and carried by more of them supporting the floats' immense weight. A little later Maxwell rang me and said that he could not get away from the Ritz, as he had a row on his hands with the unions in the *Daily Mirror* and could not leave the telephone. I said this did not matter to me, I was coming down that way in any case on other business (the other business was in fact to get my hair cut by the barber at the Ritz, the foremost expert in his trade). So I drove to the Ritz Hotel, and at the front door was greeted by a polite young man who took me to Maxwell's suite. Maxwell greeted me at the door with great courtesy wearing a smart and well-cut pinstripe suit, but with no shoes or socks on. Not long afterwards, he pointed at his large, gnarled, naked feet and said, 'Sorry about all this.' No further explanation appeared necessary or forthcoming, and I regret to this day that I did not ask him what was wrong with his feet and why he was padding about without shoes and socks on. He then engaged me in a monologue which largely turned upon the deal he hoped to make with between the Polanco

164

Group and the Mirror Group, and the conversations he had had with the King and the Spanish Prime Minister, giving me the impression that we were on the brink of a vast and important merger of the British and Spanish media. I listened to this with my mouth half open, it never crossing my mind that for at least part of the time I was listening to the ravings of a megalomaniac.

He said he had had a number of conversations with the King and Felipe González, and every so often his telephone rang and he spoke to someone in his office in London (was it Peter Jay?) in terms which seemed to me highly offensive. When, after an hour or so, I left him he padded with me along to the lift in the hotel, still shoeless and sockless. I do not think his visit yielded any very important results although *El Pais*, the main newspaper owned by Polanco, carried a piece about it in its issue of the next day.

The King was mystified by the whole business. I met him at a reception a couple of days later, and he beckoned me over. 'Who is this Maxwell fellow who keeps ringing me up?' he asked. Maxwell's office in his suite in the Ritz Hotel was a hive of activity, with harassed typists and so on rushing about doing whatever he told them to do. When I left him I still had no clear idea of what he intended, and I am not sure he did either. His powers of persuasion were immense, and I think that when I left him I would have believed almost everything he told me, whether I understood it or not. He was introduced to me by a young Spanish lobbyist on the fringe of politics named Antonio Eraso, who had also been instrumental in introducing me to the property tycoon Gerald Ronson, a few weeks earlier. I was always on the lookout in case Antonio, a fixer and intriguer, introduced me to more picturesque characters of this kind, but for some reason he decided to stop at two. On the whole, I was grateful that he did.

I missed, rather to my disappointment (it was between

165

my two postings to Madrid), the abortive right-wing coup d'état run by the absurd Mayor Tejero, of the Guardia Civil, when shots were fired in the Cortes by Tejero's supporters backed by some supporting army elements who wished to turn Spain backwards, abolishing democracy and substituting a Franco-type regime. You can still see bullet holes in the walls of the Cortes, where Tejero and his men fired warning shots. The King, wisely advised by his staff, gripped the problem and dressed in his army uniform spoke to the nation on television. In effect, he said he had no sympathy with the would-be rebels, and that the nation should rally behind him, which they did. Tejero was duly arrested and put in prison. I am told that the extreme right-wing aunt of a friend of mine wished to see him to congratulate and commiserate with him on his failed attempt to secure a Franco-type restoration, with the army and a tame king replacing Spain's new democracy. She duly presented herself at the guard room of the prison of Alcala-Meco, only to be told, 'I am very sorry, Señora; Major Tejero only receives on Tuesdays.'

I must also include a word on 'El Duende', an untranslatable name associated in some way with magical powers. El Duende was a sort of one-man car call-up system in Madrid. If there was a large embassy or other grand cocktail party, as there frequently was, El Duende would turn up, uninvited, help the cars to park, assist the important passengers to alight, and put them back in their cars when the party was over, receiving a small but discreet tip of a few pesetas for his trouble. It was not always a courteous service. If an ambassador was late, El Duende rarely let them pass without comment. 'Late again, I see, Ambassador,' was one of his mildest observations.

Rafael was our chauffeur for our first few years in Madrid. He was teetotal on (he said) the doctor's instructions many years ago. I was surprised one day when on the way to the embassy I noticed a strong smell of alcohol. I tackled Rafael about this. 'It is not me who is drinking,' I said. 'It must be you.' Rafael denied this with indignation. No one else could be responsible. It was a dialogue of the deaf. Eventually Rafael said he *never* touched a drop of alcohol. Of course he sometimes had a glass or two of wine before driving me to work but alcohol never. This nonplussed me and I let the matter drop, never having before drawn a distinction between alcohol and wine. Neither of us referred to the matter again. My conclusion was that Rafael's drinking regime suited both him and me well. His alcohol intake remained moderate, happy in his belief that he never touched drink, and it relaxed him for tackling Madrid traffic and its frequent jams. I used in the end to ease my way through Madrid traffic, when driving, by taking a slug or two of vino tinto before starting the journey. Rafael never commented on this either. Nor did I, though some guests must have had the feeling of being driven around in a mobile pub.

When Rafael retired, we gave a party for him and about a dozen other ambassadorial chauffeurs, including the dignified gentlemen who drove for the papal nuncio, and the Venezuelan ambassador's chauffeur who was dean of the Ambassadorial Chauffeurs Corps. Rafael's wife was present and wept copiously throughout the long and, I think, eloquent speeches made by Rafael, the Venezuelan and myself. We also invited some very grand grandees who knew Rafael, among them the Marquesa de Santa Cruz, the Condesa de Toreno and others. It was a moving occasion with much emotion. El Duende turned up rather late with his small transistor radio in his pocket, its volume full on. Someone asked him why he had brought his radio with him to the party, and El Duende said he had done so because he feared he might be bored.

Then there was Miss Hibbs, who was English and nanny to Franco's family for many years, which meant in practice looking after Franco's grandchildren, the children of the

Marquesa de Villaverde, his only child. Mary met Miss Hibbs at a children's party shortly after our arrival, in 1966, and said that we had an English nanny – much younger – with us ourselves. Miss Hibbs, widely known in Spain as the 'Nanissima', said firmly, 'I shall come and call on her.' A few days later we were surprised by a black Rolls-Royce entering our little drive, accompanied by two policemen on motor bicycles. Out stepped Miss Hibbs, with a very small boy with large liquid brown eyes holding her hand. After introducing herself, she said (in English) to Franco's youngest grandson, 'Say good morning, Francisco, there's a good boy.' She added in an undertone to me in a nanny voice: 'Just like his grandfather, that's what I always say.'

She was firm with Franco, not allowing him, for instance, to take little Francisco with him on a day's shooting, on the grounds that he was too small; and she would not budge. Franco called her 'his personal Gibraltar'. The grandchildren were kind and good to her, especially when she was old and infirm, and took her for walks in her wheelchair. When I saw Miss Hibbs I always used to ask her about Franco's health, which was of obvious political interest in determining the future of Spain. Miss Hibbs was always quite frank. 'I am afraid the Generalissimo is not at all himself this morning,' she would say, but Franco was physically robust and lived for a further eight or nine years after we had arrived in Spain. Like most diplomats I only met Franco a few times, and then only to shake his hand on some formal occasion.

It was different for Charlie Wiggin, whom I have earlier mentioned as my predecessor in Washington, and who became ambassador to Spain a few years later. After he had been in Spain for a short while, he presented his credentials to Franco, as all new ambassadors did. After formally handing over the relevant letter from the Queen, he and Franco went and sat in a small room in the royal palace for a chat, rather as I did some years later with the King and Fernando Moran.

But whereas on the latter occasion we had a friendly chat, Charlie Wiggin's meeting with Franco began with an icy silence. Eventually, Charles – whose Spanish was fluent – said to Franco, 'We have one thing in common, Generalissimo. We are both very fond of fishing in the rivers of Asturias.' There was another long silence. 'That,' said Franco, 'is the *only* thing we have in common' – a rather dispiriting start to Charles's ambassadorial career.

Franco's silences, which became increasingly frequent with his old age, were always awkward ones. The King, on the other hand, liked gossiping, and when we met he would talk about whatever concerned him at the time, half in Spanish and half in English. He was often alarmingly indiscreet, and there were some things which I still wish he had not told me. But he seemed to know whom he trusted and would never have told me some of the things he did if he thought I would pass them on to people who ought not to know them. My friend, the American ambassador, a highly professional career diplomat, found the same thing. (His predecessor, Thomas Enders, had been under-secretary for Latin America during the Falklands War, and profoundly unhelpful to us.) The King was not only jolly but a formidable judge of people including his own ministers. On more than one occasion, in the sixties, he told me that this or that minister was the one to watch for the future as they had more ability than the rest. In each case he turned out to be right. He especially admired Fernandez Miranda, who played a key role in the restoration of the monarchy. Later on, his chief regard was for a youthful and intelligent young man called Eduardo Serra, a fair-minded technocrat who was a junior minister in Franco's government and a full minister under the Democratic government which followed his death. Eduardo belonged to no political party. He was efficient and conscientious. I used to see him frequently about arms sales and seek his informal advice about almost anything else.

169

He always gave me straight answers and was always good company. He was an especially good friend of Tristan Garel-Jones, a deputy chief whip in the Conservative Party who for many years owned the English teaching school which his father had founded in Madrid.

When I went to see the King, at his request or mine, it was usually a memorable occasion. His house (it was a house rather than a palace) was three or four miles away from where I lived, in the middle of a large estate covered in scrub and a forest of trees of the type the Spaniards call *encinas* – a form of dwarf oak. Rafael would always drive me to these interviews slowly, not just because there was a strictly upheld speed limit, but because in the winter we had to slow down to avoid the wild boar in his park, which had come down from the frozen and snow-covered Guadarrama Mountains in search of the food, which they had failed to find at a higher level.

There were other families who were never closely associated with the government but who became real friends. There was the Urquijo family. Jaime Urquijo was a successful and respected businessman, whose real love was for country pursuits – riding and shooting – and the wildlife of all kinds at his estate about an hour away from Madrid. His wife, nicknamed 'Piru', for reasons too complex to spell out here, was a phenomenon. She had a degree in psychology and spoke English, German, French and, of course, Spanish with equal fluency and could be very funny in all of them. She knew absolutely everyone in Madrid. Her grandfather was the great Spanish polymath Gregorio Marañon, who as well as being professor of medicine of great repute was also an historian, author and philanthropist with a multitude of friends from all backgrounds and classes. Like him, 'Piru' had time for everyone including her six children, and an energy and intelligence which matched that of Mrs Thatcher. She also had a brilliant sense of humour. I was instrumental in helping to make her the president of Sotheby's in Spain, but I felt that Sotheby's never sufficiently appreciated her knowledge or contacts or her many other qualities – she was and is unique.

There were many other groups of friends who, perhaps with less influence as public figures, wielded great influence and proved constant friends throughout. One such was the Marques de Perinat, the director general in the Spanish foreign ministry in the sixties, in charge of relationships with America, and especially the American air bases in Spain, which were a point of great sensitivity in the relations between the two countries. A humorous and quirky person, with a beautiful wife, we saw them a lot socially and one year spent two weeks exploring Scotland with them. To our delight, he was not long afterwards made ambassador to London where he enjoyed himself and was liked. He had a good sense of fun. On our joint holiday to Scotland we visited a number of stately homes where the owners were uniformly kind and generous. Many of them had never met Spaniards before and were enchanted by the manners and friendliness of the Perinats. The elegant chatelaine of one stately home we visited approached Luis Guillermo, we having just arrived by car shortly before lunch time, and asked discreetly if he would like to make himself comfortable before luncheon was served. Luis Guillermo was mystified. 'What is this "Make yourself comfortable" thing?' he asked me in an undertone. I explained that his distinguished hostess was in fact asking him if wanted to pee before lunch or not. 'Ah!' said Luis Guillermo. The next day, on our travels again throughout Scotland we searched for a good place to have a picnic. I found a wonderful site, on the edge of a strikingly beautiful loch. 'Well, here we are!' I said. 'Here is an ideal place for our picnic, and I will start to unpack the hamper.' 'No,' said Luis Guillermo. 'We cannot have our picnic here. A cow has very recently made itself comfortable there.'

171

Then there was the Argüelles family, who had a long history of distinction in Spanish public and cultural affairs. The head of the family and his many children had all been in the Spanish Embassy in London through the Blitz in World War II. This meant that they understood us, and that their sympathies were Anglophile. His wife was the first lady ever to become a diplomat in Spain and was intelligent and amusing. His large and very talented family included bankers, artists, sculptors, architects, the director of the Royal Opera company (and ex-private secretary to the Queen). He himself had a career which had comprised politics, banking and diplomacy. He ended his public career as Spanish ambassador in Washington. I painted a lot with his immensely talented second daughter, Marga, who had huge artistic ability, even though she appeared to have received no formal training whatsoever. She has had several highly successful painting exhibitions in Madrid and London, and her eldest son is now one of Spain's most distinguished portrait painters. Don Jaime was a true old-fashioned gentleman, the sort of person you hoped you would find in a foreign country, with a strong sense of humour and an understanding of strange and curious foreigners such as ourselves.

Meanwhile Gibraltar continued to arouse indignation, largely from people – Spanish or British – who were wholly ignorant of the subject or its history, with the Gibraltarians as the chief troublemakers, which frustrated me as much as it did José Joaquin Puig, my Spanish opposite number. So we thought the best we could do was to concentrate on the positive areas of our relations, leaving the Gibraltarians to stew in their own juice. This was a policy upon which we both embarked with a deliberate intent. It will take a number of years before the Gibraltarian dispute becomes any less difficult to handle. All I can say is that Puig and I did our best to divert attention towards the good parts of our relationship, and to ignore the parts like Gibraltar which got in the way of it. Puig and his wife were very agreeable people who had very many close friends in England. He was an exceptional ambassador – always loyal to his own government, but quick to discern ways in which he could improve the relationship with Britain. His most heroic act had nothing to do with diplomacy. He and his wife had laid on a large and extremely grand dinner party for the Prince and Princess of Wales at his embassy in London. On the day of the dinner party, he developed symptoms which his doctor correctly diagnosed as an acute appendicitis. He sat through the dinner party, with the doctor, who was a mutual friend of both of ours, included as an extra guest. Immediately the Waleses had left after dinner, Puig, accompanied by the doctor, raced to hospital where his appendix was successfully removed. It was not an evening which he remembers with great pleasure.

Somewhere in this book I must pay tribute to the Kinnocks. Neil and his family were good friends of Felipe González, the Spanish Prime Minister, and his wife. Felipe had invited them as friends, and their two teenage children, for a few days' holiday in Spain – a real holiday without talks or formal occasions. It was completely unofficial; neither I nor the embassy was involved, all I did was meet them on arrival, and deliver them to their hotel, which, as luck would have it, was very near our house. On the last day of their visit we got a message from the Spanish airport authorities to say that there was a report of a bomb on board the Kinnocks' aircraft, and that the aircraft, by now well on its way home, would have to return to Spain. We met the Kinnocks when they landed again at Madrid Airport (there was in the event no bomb) and took them back to the embassy for dinner, the two children contenting themselves with snacks in their hotel. They were calm and amusing and admirably uncomplaining throughout. They were grateful for the sympathy they received, but wanted no publicity. They took a later flight home. Neil Kinnock was his usual cheerful and talkative self, accompanied only by Charles Clarke – now Minister of Education in the present government. We packed them off to the airport again after dinner, Neil still talkative and Glenys Kinnock looking as pretty as she normally did. They expressed great gratitude and we all felt that the whole family had emerged from an unpleasant ordeal with courage and dignity. I knew nothing of what went on in the conversations between Neil Kinnock and Felipe González. I expect it touched on Labour Party politics and European Socialism, both subjects dear to the heart of Neil Kinnock, upon both of which he was inclined to talk for a very long time indeed. I was grateful for the opportunity of meeting them both and thought it a good move for the heads of the Labour Parties in each country to meet on an entirely informal and friendly basis, with no pomp, no formality and no set agenda.

21

Security

There has always been what we would now call a security problem between the English and Spanish. Trade rivalries always played a large part in this, and other factors arising from Spain's wealth and vulnerability and European dynastic problems, as well as, of course, since the early eighteenth century, Gibraltar. But above all there has been the religious divide, the Protestant English fearful of the conspiratorial influence of Catholicism, and the Spanish seeking to convert the English back to the Catholic faith. The latter has been, from the end of the sixteenth century until comparatively recently, an object of Spanish policy, and the English college in Valladolid is still going. From the time of the Spanish Armada, this seminary has been training young English priests for the Catholic priesthood and still does so, the object being to strengthen the entrants into the Catholic Church in England with a view to converting the Protestant population back to the true faith. There is also in Valladolid a slightly later Scottish seminary with the same objective and view. It is an intriguing thought that for over 400 years many English and Scottish Catholic priests will have received their early training, which is a tough one, in Valladolid. The permanent staff in both seminaries consist of a handful of ordained priests and monks, and the places have the feel of small universities about them. In the last war, it did some good work for Britain in looking after British prisoner-of-war escapees, and acted as a source of information on the military activities of the Germans.

Over the years there have been many conspiracies mounted on either side. In my time there were a good many Irishmen in Spain, by no means all lovers of Britain. Many felt a bond with Spaniards in their Catholicism, and there were a few on the extreme wing on either side who cooperated over planning violence, or at least on logistics, with ETA or the IRA. ETA, the initials of which stand for Basque words which I would not dare to translate, was mostly composed of violent youths, well trained in terrorism sometimes by each other and sometimes by extreme terrorist elements in the Middle East. We were very conscious of these people and the menace they represented. One day, I got a note from ETA (for some reason, so did my German and Japanese opposite numbers) in which there was a threat to kill us. I forget the reason; I think it was something to do with our support for capitalism. I handed the note to the Spanish security service, who obligingly supplied me with new and bogus licence plates for my cars, which my son and his friends had much pleasure in screwing on. A few days later, a senior Spanish security officer rang me up and said, 'It is all right, the note you got was not from ETA.' I observed that it was obviously sent from someone who did not like me much but the Spanish security people appeared to attach little importance to this.

They took the threat more seriously when I said I would like to visit the Basque Country, the centre of ETA activity. The extreme Basque nationalists were people who wished to see the Basque territory independent of Spain, and they used a number of measures to help them in this aim. One was the protection money racket, many prosperous Basque companies paying the ETA money to protect them from being attacked. At its most extreme, the ETA used assassination as a weapon. Their targets were not foreigners or tourists, but usually members of the Spanish armed forces or the Guardia Civil, whose job it was to hunt them down, and the more senior the person they could kill the better, although sometimes – rather like the IRA – they seemed a little vague about their human targets, and vaguer still about the general policy they wanted to follow and the kind of society they wished to bring about. At one level they were, or seemed to me to be, completely mad. A Basque nation including the Basque provinces of France was never a realistic objective, and they had neither the organisation nor the political experience to build any institutional structure.

The Basque police were on the whole very efficient. They took my death threat more seriously when I visited the Basque Country – Bilbao, San Sebastián, etc. – getting there by driving with Rafael, my chauffeur, along the autoroute marking the border between old Castille and the Basque Country. As we approached the frontier of the Basque Country there was a barrier-cum-tollgate where all cars had to stop and pay something to get through to the other side. There, on the border, was a filthy saloon car with three dirty unshaven men inside wearing beads, their faces full of menace. They accompanied Mary and me and Rafael in our car throughout the visit, being, as they were, well-disguised bodyguards who were members of the local Basque police force. When the time came to say goodbye to them the chief of the detachment said, 'You need a new car, Ambassador. With your present one you cannot accelerate out of trouble fast enough.' Rafael approved of this. I think he had a vision of a bright new gleaming super-fast car which the Foreign Office would send us, but of course he was disappointed and all we got in the end was a Jaguar with bullet-proof windows, and that only a few months before I left.

I do not know if my predecessors as ambassador in the nineteenth-century Spanish Peninsular War (in Spain known as the War of Independence) were also threatened – I expect they were, as the casualties and carnage in that war were horrific. One day, the local correspondent of the *Daily Mail* (a friend named Tim Brown) telephoned me. The Ministry of Public Works was working on a bypass road around the bottleneck town of Talavera de la Reina, and the diggers had uncovered a very large quantity of human bones. These were clearly the remains of the English and French as well as Spanish soldiers killed there, amounting to a total of killed, wounded or missing on the British side of over 5,000 and on the French side just over 7,000. Figures included troops from other countries fighting mostly on our side, namely Portuguese, Germans and, of course, Spanish. In a nice gesture of respect, and in cooperation with our own Ministry of Defence, the Spanish built a monument to the dead in this battle which you pass by on the road from Madrid to Portugal. A Spaniard whom I met there one weekend had dug up several buttons on the site, belonging to an English regiment of lancers, only a few inches below the surface. These were brave members of a regiment who, in pursuit of the retreating French, had failed to notice a ditch which had unhorsed many of their men galloping after their adversaries. It was a pursuit which Wellington later on criticised, on the grounds that his cavalry commanders had insufficient control over their troops.

Then there was the major security event of my time in Madrid, which was the abortive attempt by the IRA to blow up the band of the Gibraltar Regiment and its spectators, and the Governor, when they were having their little ceremonial parade in the main square of Gibraltar just opposite the Governor's residence. The intention was, of course, to secure a propaganda victory and to kill as many people as possible. There is a lot that could be said about this operation and the way in which it was frustrated. This will no doubt one day be the subject of a separate essay or

178

another book. Suffice it to say, on this occasion our own security people received the greatest possible cooperation from the Spanish police, who had as much interest in the spread of terrorism in Spain as we did. There was a great relief all round when, in an underground car park in Marbella, a car rented by the IRA terrorists was found to contain a huge quantity of explosives. All the terrorists, who were found to have no arms or weapons on them at the time, were subsequently shot dead. The Spanish Foreign Minister telephoned me when he heard the first news about this. 'The thought occurred to me,' he said, 'that if only the car could have been driven to Gibraltar and the Rock sort of towed out to sea for a short distance then the whole problem might, well...' He did not expect me to comment on this, and I did not. But it was clear that, like many of his compatriots, he earnestly wished that the problem of Gibraltar would somehow go away and that the removal of the Rock in its entirety would be a good way of doing this.

The main problem after the events in Gibraltar was the inquest conducted entirely independently, in which witnesses to the shootings were interrogated by the coroner and a vote was taken on the conclusions. It was clear to all concerned what had happened and that the IRA team had acted with murderous intent, and when the vote came at the end of the coroner's court proceedings, the SAS troops who were involved in the action against the terrorists were cleared. But there were some anxious moments. The saddest aspect of the whole business was when my opposite number in Gibraltar, Air Marshal Sir Peter Terry, retired to England and the IRA attempted to murder him and his wife at home. They did not succeed, but they injured him severely. All he was doing was his duty, which he fulfilled admirably well, and the attempt to assassinate him achieved nothing. The incident also proved the IRA's capability for acting independently and their professional capability for mounting violent operations overseas.

A few weeks later, after my death threat, on my way to work, Antonio, my driver, took off from the house at enormous speed taking corners on two wheels and not stopping until he reached the comparative security of the embassy compound. I asked him what the hell was going on, and he said that he was being followed by a car which looked to him very suspicious and he felt it right to accelerate fast away from it. I took this up with the Spanish security officials too, only to discover from them that there had been some monumental mix up, and they had been following my car under the impression that it was somehow involved with the terrorist movement. There must have been red faces all round when it was discovered that my Spanish police escort had got it the wrong way round, but I never heard any more about this incident again.

Talking of bombs makes me recall an incident that took place much earlier in my life. We had one bomb at Goodwood, in early 1944, on our return home from the USA. It landed on our side of the road dividing the Goodwood Estate from that of Mr Edward James (the eccentric son of the notorious society hostess mentioned by Hilaire Belloc in his poem ending: 'and Mrs James will entertain the King'). The bomb made a huge hole and, although two miles away from Goodwood House, broke a number of windows there. My mother (it was about midnight) rushed to see if Charles and I were all right, which of course we were, only sleepy. The bomb seemed to have been jettisoned from a German bomber – you could tell from its deep engine note. Having carried out its raid on a more strategic target, it was presumably shedding its weight and therefore increasing its speed, on its way home to its base. The bomb made Charles and me feel rather less like war funks who had fled (albeit briefly) to America. Curiously enough, we did not receive as many of the 'war funk' taunts which were aimed at many of our fellow evacuees, and which upset them quite a lot. I think that a lot of our own contemporaries were jealous of us and our adventure.

No sooner had we gone, a few months later, to Eton than there were more bombs, this time the German pilot-less V1 'flying bombs'. These flew rather slowly towards their targets, and when they were roughly overhead the engine cut out and the bomb descended, the normal time between engine cut-off and the explosion was 10–20 seconds, giving us boys little time to grab our slippers, dressing gowns and gas masks before going down to the air-raid shelter in the garden where there were tiers of concrete bunk beds with blankets on them on which you slept, or were at least meant to, until the 'all clear' siren sounded. But sleep was achieved with difficulty because the thugs and oafs in the House, and there were plenty of these, sang as many obscene songs as they could remember or played cards (these were the ones who could barely read or write, and I suspect probably went direct from Eton to their respective regiments such as the Life Guards, where academic distinction was not an urgent requirement).

The smallest boys, as a result of the flying bombs, were desperately short of rest and at Early School the next day there were always little boys asleep with their desks used as pillows for their heads. The beaks were very tolerant of this. More tragically, there were little boys who had lost fathers or brothers in action in the war. One such was my little cousin Henry Vyner, who wept inconsolably when his elder sister (a trainee nurse) died from encephalitis and his elder brother, a pilot in the Fleet Air Army, crashed into the sea during the Burma Campaign. But Henry had panache in large quantities and was a clever boy, and soon concentrated

181

on a life of pleasure which involved drink and gambling and much jollity. He was much loved, and I have always taken the view that he should have received a special grant for cheering people up and for his generosity, which ultimately took the form of a large and ill-concealed cocktail party which led to his departure from Eton rather earlier than the majority of his contemporaries (and guests). He was a hero to me then and still is now. I later shared a flat with him in Mayfair, occasionally moving elsewhere when he had one of his more raucous gambling parties. I had to work the next morning, Henry's rich friends did not. A very great deal of money changed hands, by no means all of it coming in Henry's direction.

Under the loose heading of security I must include a brief word, admittedly out of context, about my friends in the CIA, with whom I worked in close contact in the Whitehall intelligence community after my first spell in Spain. There were about six of them, not assassins but intelligence analysts. I took them to Goodwood in the main Goodwood Race Week in mid-summer. Being trained analysts, the form book, *Time Form*, and all the other statistical information and other data to indicate the winning horses held no mysteries for them. After greeting my brother politely on alighting from their minibus, they applied themselves to the available literature and each made comfortable sums of money. They returned happy agents to Whitehall the next week, and I felt I had contributed something special to the Anglo-American relationship.

22

State Visits

I must have had a hand in more state visits than most of my Foreign Service contemporaries. The first was the one made by the Queen to the USA in 1957, then one by the Queen to Spain in 1986 and one by the King of Spain to England (he stayed at Windsor Castle) in 1988. I think we had official visits in Spain from all the other adult members of the royal family, except Princess Margaret and the Princes Andrew and Edward. The Duke of Gloucester came with a party of structural engineers; the Duke of Kent came with a party of senior businessmen intent on boosting exports. The Duke of Wellington had the Queen Mother to stay privately, just after I had retired; and the Prince and Princess of Wales came for a three- or four-day visit as guests of the King, at whose guest palace they stayed. Before these visits, the contacts between the two royal families had been few and far between. Now, the Spanish royals have become fairly frequent informal visitors to London, having cousins – including the Queen's brother (the King of Greece) – living there together with other relations from other monarchies or ex-monarchies in exile.

State visits tend to follow traditional and routine lines, and their programmes, looked at after the event, make boring reading. On our side, the Lord Chamberlain's Office take charge of the planning, drawing on their deep experience. I have often reflected on what these visits really achieved. First, they normally improve, even if temporarily, the atmosphere in which normal business and all other forms of collaboration between the two countries are conducted, although they do not help much in solving intractable bilateral problems (for example, Gibraltar). They thicken up the personal relationship between heads of state even if these concern free countries with strong links already in existence between them. They help to promote the international stability which we all seek. They are a great excuse for cultural and artistic exchanges, for media coverage, memorable ceremonial events and lavish parties. The participants, especially the sort who like ceremony and dressing up, normally enjoy them greatly; the planners and organisers rather less, because of the detailed and exhausting planning involved in advance. Some state visits must be a crashing bore for our own Royal Family or even worse (imagine having the Ceauşescus of Romania on your hands as house guests for several days). The principal guests are normally accompanied by a large entourage. Private secretaries, equerries and ADCs, the Foreign Secretary and some of his staff, press officers, footmen, baggage handlers, secretaries and even on our side an official called the Travelling Yeoman. His duties were never clear to me, but he was fond of a drink when he could get one, which seemed to be quite often. Additionally, of course, there are policemen, chefs, valets and a doctor; and not least, the ambassador, often with a very small staff, doing all the planning, increasingly swamped by all the detailed preparation, but a little more relaxed once the visit has started and acquired a momentum of its own. That is the human element. In addition, the Queen would bring with her a full dinner service for the banquet she was to offer her hosts, a great many presents for the latter and their staff and many medals to give to the people involved on the host nation's side.

*　*　*

On her visit to Spain in 1988 the Queen had a full and busy programme.

Seville turned out to be a bit of a disappointment. An outbreak of equine fever meant that the Andalusian horse extravaganza planned meticulously by the Domecq family had to be cancelled. The Spaniards, however, have a great ability to improvise, and the people of Seville in particular are *muy festivaleros* or great party people. In place of the horse extravaganza, to which we were all looking forward, a special programme of Spanish dancing was laid on in the Alhambra in Seville – not merely flamenco, but more of a medley of traditional dancing and music. It was cheerful, but like many other gatherings in Spain went on rather too long. It was a hot afternoon, and the King's eyes closed at one particular moment, which was of course the moment captured on film, but it attracted little attention in the press, and the King was not the only one in the party to be overcome by drowsiness.

The sight of the Queen entering the vast cathedral in Seville, past Columbus's tomb, the organ playing our national anthem flat out, and the huge and magnificent Archbishop and Cardinal Amigo welcoming her with outstretched arms was one to remember. Sevillans liked to shout compliments (*piropos*) at women, and I remember one man in the crowd when there was a comparatively quiet moment, shouting, 'How come you haven't invited any ugly people to this?'

Leaving Seville, we flew on to Barcelona in an aircraft of the Queen's Flight. It was a very hot day. The Queen and Prince Philip were sitting on seats facing each other on one side of the aisle, reading. Across the aisle, there were four seats with Mary and me and the Howes in them. We were all very busy in one way or another, and I was writing a few words for the Queen to deliver on her departure from Spain in a few days' time. I had taken off my jacket and

185

had braces underneath, the sort which clip on rather than attaching themselves to buttons. At one moment, all the clip-on attachments to the braces popped and came undone leaving my trousers with no support. No one paid much attention to this except the Queen who looked up from her book briefly and said, 'Emotion?' I had no ready quip in answer to this, but Geoffrey Howe, with his usual kindness and tact, explained that this happened to him constantly too, and that braces with buttons were the only reliable thing to have.

We had a heavy programme in Barcelona with all the indispensable formal engagements ending with a cocktail party on the Royal Yacht *Britannia*, which had sailed there from England, with the Royal Marine band marching and counter-marching on the quayside to the delight of a growing group of Catalans. The yacht had been cleared of furniture to make room for more guests, as our own residence in Madrid had been two days previously, to make room for the Queen to receive the diplomatic corps accredited to Spain. On entering the Royal Yacht, the Queen said to Mary, 'You see, no furniture, just like your house.' Just before the party, the Spanish ambassador and I had tried to get all our hosts and guests to visit Barcelona's old and handsome theatre, the Liceu, which had a marvellous picture collection inside it and had been largely rebuilt following a fire (the pictures by noted Catalan artists were saved). We were confident that we could get someone like Placido Domingo or Monserrat Caballé to sing if the royal party came. The two monarchs, however, felt that this was far too much, the programme being crowded enough as it was. 'Do you want to kill us all?' asked the King, with Prince Philip in support. After a short argument, which the Spanish ambassador and I inevitably lost, it was decided that the day would end with a cocktail party on the Royal Yacht, with everyone who was anyone in Barcelona present.

But the cocktail party on the Royal Yacht did not mark the end of the festivities. The two royal families had agreed that after the formal state visit ended they would have a private family picnic on board the Royal Yacht in Mallorca, in the Port of Palma. It was indeed a very private affair, those present being the immediate circle of courtiers accompanying our own royal party and their Spanish opposite numbers, few in numbers. I think Mary and I were the only outsiders present.

It had some unusual touches. First, it was the first and only barbecue we had ever attended on board a ship. Dress was decreed to be informal, though the word 'informal' left the ladies present in a turmoil of uncertainty. The men wore no ties, and certainly no uniforms, and Cdr Tim Lawrence, later to marry the Princess Royal as her second husband, was present as Equerry to the Queen. Prince Philip, who was something of an expert at barbecues, did the preparation, cooking and carving, the ladies handed round the vegetables and salads. There was no placement and we all sat on benches and helped ourselves from trestle tables. It was a merry occasion, and the barbecue delicious. The barbecue sauce was momentarily lost by Prince Philip and only found when a Royal Yacht steward, in a white tie, formal uniform and medals, emerged from the body of the Yacht, and found it in a drawer in the elaborate contraption Prince Philip used for his barbecue making.

The party then broke up, the Spaniards making the short trip to the King's ultra-modern yacht (a gift, I think, from an Arab prince) and we all settled for an early bed after what had been – even by state visit standards – an exhausting programme.

But this was still not the last we saw of the Royal Yacht. The Queen Mother wanted one last trip in it before it was decommissioned. This was even more private. Her guests were Lady Grimthorpe, Michael Oswald, who ran the Queen

Mother's stud and his wife, Gerald Ward and his wife Amanda, Alastair Aird, the Queen Mother's private secretary; a full crew and a detachment (including band) of the Royal Marines. We started in Portsmouth, called at a new refinery on the Solent, visited a particularly fine garden near Falmouth, and gave a cocktail party for the Cornish great and good. The Queen Mother entertained the ship's officers, whatever their seniority, at dinner every night, one sitting on either side of her. The whole trip took about three days and nights. During the warm weather, I sat on the deck next to the Queen Mother painting the Channel coast, while Gerald Ward provided endless and entertaining gossip as we headed east for Portsmouth and home.

On the way, we passed the RN Destroyer HMS *Richmond* and exchanged messages with my brother, who for some reason happened to be a guest aboard. These were the pompous things vessels send each other when they pass each other at sea. HMS *Richmond* was very fast and looked menacing and my money would have been on HMS *Richmond* had the two vessels come to blows. I doubt if the Queen Mother saw our exchange; but she was too polite to admit it if she had done.

The state visit was successful despite what the Spaniards would have called an 'exchange of views' between Prince Philip and Eduardo Sanchez-Junco, the editor of *Hola* magazine, parent of the magazine *Hello* in English. Prince Philip, who I doubt could read much of the Spanish *Hola*, accused Eduardo Sanchez in fairly intemperate terms of intrusive and offensive journalism. 'Ho, just like *Paris Match*, I suppose,' he said sarcastically. Eduardo's English was shaky, and I hoped he had not detected the tone of the prince's remarks. There was a bad moment when Eduardo's wife, whose English was very fluent, appeared, as I feared a row. Fortunately others joined us, and the group became enlarged. I was much relieved. Eduardo Sanchez was a nice, polite person. He was doing his best to demonstrate his sympathy with the British royal family and I liked him a lot.

The Queen accepted the busy programme and all it involved with her usual serenity. Prince Philip, on the other hand, especially when in Barcelona, became rather impatient with the massive traffic jams which he encountered, which he attributed to local police attempts to clear and speed up traffic for the royal convoy. I tried to tell him that Barcelona traffic was always like this on a normal day, but I doubt if he believed me, and he did not resume his calm for a while.

There were more relaxed moments as well as pomp and circumstance. In between formal visits to the offices of the mayor and Generalitat (local government in Barcelona) which are on opposite sides of the same square, the King broke away from his guests to go into a little street bakery to help himself to a delicious fried *churro* which Spaniards like to eat with their breakfast coffee. This simple piece of shoplifting went down well with the large crowd which had by then gathered, and the baker of the *churro* was of course a very happy person too. At about this time there was also an explosion in the square – not a large one so I took it to be a *feu de joie*, but it turned out to have been a little protest by a small pro-independence Catalan movement. No one, except the odd policeman, paid the slightest attention.

On the last day of the state visit, there was also some restrained but jolly informality at the end of the large official luncheon which the city of Barcelona gave for the Queen and Prince Philip. There were speeches of course, but these were followed by the guests (or those who wanted to) rising and dancing the sardana, the stately but melodious Catalan dance which bears some relation to 'Ring a Ring of Roses', though without the 'All fall down' at the end. To my recollection not just the royal principals joined in, but drivers and policemen too. It was a happy occasion.

Barcelona is the perfect place for a state visit. Lively and busy, with sophisticated shops and theatres, excellent restaurants, animated but serious-minded people, marvellous mad buildings (like Gaudi's cathedral), wonderful picture collections, the Ramblas with its population of respectable stall-holders selling anything you want, together with three-card trick experts, pickpockets and prostitutes, geese (for some obscure historical reason living in the old cathedral cloisters), blocks of flats with spacious and elaborate roof gardens, and, of course, the Barcelona football team, rather like the Catholic Church in the devotion it arouses. The mayor in my time was a poet of considerable repute; Carreras and Caballé were singing like angels; and we all felt it a pity that our royal party could not spend more time in Barcelona to hear them sing.

The moments of informality enjoyed by the British royals in Spain could not have happened, or were most unlikely to have done so, in England, even if something as delicious as *churros* had been available there at little roadside bakeries. Before the Spanish state visit to England in 1988 Mary and I went to London and had a long and detailed meeting with the Lord Chamberlain's officials in London to go over their minutely prepared programme. When asked if we had any questions, I asked where to look in the programme for the moment of 'planned spontaneity' (there had been talk of the King visiting a supermarket or somewhere similar with no prior warning in advance). A chill descended on the meeting. 'We all strongly hope,' said the Lord Chamberlain's representative, 'that there will be nothing of that kind.' So there wasn't.

Back to the private picnic. As the Royal Yacht left, to the accompaniment of a massive fireworks display which the Queen thought was as good as anything she had seen in

Hong Kong, we all relaxed. The yacht moored off Palma the next morning. There we were surrounded by a number of motor yachts of the 'gin palace' variety, many of them clearly hired by British tourists, with their compliment of large bikini-wearing ladies of a certain age on board with binoculars trained on the *Britannia* to see what was going on there. Not much was. We looked back through our own binoculars at them.

It had been agreed that the Spanish King and Queen would take our own royal couple, perhaps with a police car or two, on a little tour of Mallorca, driving up the spectacularly mountainous and beautiful west coast via the pretty village of Valldemossa and its Carthusian monastery, now owned by the Carvajal family who were close friends of ours. This was the place where Chopin and Georges Sand had such a miserable holiday nearly 150 years before, the climate and the local inhabitants both making life unpleasant for them. It had been arranged that our Queen's own senior entourage, including Mary and me, about 20 of us in all, would ourselves go on a bus tour following more or less the same route as the Queen and Prince Philip. There was a muddle over the Queen's departure. King Juan Carlos and Queen Sofiá arrived on the quayside, the King at the wheel of his own car, but there was no sign of life on the Royal Yacht. The King eventually spotted me on the deck and shouted to ask if anyone was at home. I scuttled off and eventually found the Queen and Prince Philip, and they and their Spanish hosts took off on their little tour.

After they had left, the courtiers – in festive mood – all assembled on the quayside. The bus that had been organised for them to take their own tour in was there all right, with the ignition key in place, but there was no driver. After waiting and failing to find him, the Queen's assistant private secretary and a Foreign Office contemporary of mine, Ken Scott, said to me, 'You're the ambassador, you know the island, you talk the language, you drive us!' So I took the wheel of the bus and off we went. I had never driven a bus before and found it exhilarating and challenging, particularly since the road to Valdemossa climbed steeply, with many hairpin bends.

As I was negotiating these, with my morale increasing, I said to my passengers, 'My next trick will be to produce the King and Queen of Spain passing us at speed on their way back to Palma.' No sooner had I said this then it happened. There was the King passing us, fast, in the opposite direction towards Palma, narrowly missing our bus. We continued on our way with the startlingly blue Mediterranean Sea beneath us on the left, had a drink somewhere and returned to have another one on the Royal Yacht before lunch (courtiers seem to live on drink). In the afternoon the Queen and Prince Philip disappeared on board, perhaps to work, perhaps to rest. I do not quite know what the King of Spain did but was later told he spent the afternoon on his own yacht, moored not far away, playing *mus*, a Spanish card game a little bit like whist, with his amiable brother-in-law Luis Gomez-Acebo, the Duke of Badajoz, who was married to his elder sister. To my great regret, neither our queen nor the Spanish king seemed to have noticed the British royal household on the bus nor the skill with which it was being driven.

Then, cocktail parties and outings being over, there was the informal barbecue held on the afterdeck of the Royal Yacht, which the few guests dressed for as informally as they dared. The party consisted of the royal visitors, the Queen of Spain's sister, Princess Irene of Greece, and one or two senior members of both royal houses. The barbecue meat was carved by Prince Philip, and the plates handed round by the Queen. The King of Spain handed round the wine, of which we all had a good deal. It was clear that he had had a very jolly time with his brother-in-law playing cards earlier in the evening.

The next morning it was all over, and the royal party got back on the Queen's Flight at Mallorca Airport. The only snag here was that someone (possibly the incredibly named Travelling Yeoman) had lost a suitcase. The King said goodbye to his royal visitors adding to me in an undertone, '*Qué alivio!*', which in English means 'What a relief!' This did not mean he had not enjoyed himself, but it did reflect the considerable strain he had no doubt felt during the visit in which he had taken the closest possible personal interest in all the detail, and which I know he was desperately anxious to have been a success. As the Queen's aircraft took off we and a small Anglo-Spanish farewell party waved goodbye, Mary throwing her hat in the air, another manifestation of '*Qué alivio!*' The Spanish press, which was present in numbers, noticed this. It was explained that it was an old Scottish custom for people to throw their hats in the air (Mary's was a Scottish-style bonnet) on occasions such as this of particular significance, and the local papers duly reported this explanation. Thus ended a long royal visit which I think the Queen and Prince Philip enjoyed, and which left us, the embassy team, nearly dead on our feet with fatigue. Mary and I left for France and spent about a week in the eastern Pyrenees restoring ourselves. We received many letters of expressions of thanks. We were all very pleased about this, but I think our main emotion, like the King's, was '*Qué alivio!*'

23

BBC

When I retired from the Foreign Office in 1990, I went, as
was customary, to say goodbye to the Foreign Secretary –
Mary's and my old friend, Douglas Hurd. We gossiped about
Spain and my time there. He then asked me whether I would
like to be a candidate for a Governorship of the BBC. The
idea seemed such a strange one that I paused a little before
accepting. I thought the job should in any case go to someone
better qualified. Then I said 'yes', reflecting that I had
already spent nearly three years being the Foreign and
Commonwealth liaison man with the World Service of the
BBC and its paymaster, that is to say the person responsible
for funding it from the Foreign Service vote, and incidentally
the person responsible for cutting its services where there
was not enough money in the vote to look after the Foreign
Office, the World Service and the British Council together.
I saw myself as doing what amounted to the exact opposite
of the job I had done at the Foreign and Commonwealth
Office some years past. I saw that among the many arguments
on this subject in the future I was likely to be squashed in
the middle, and I was not far wrong.

There were two sides to the BBC and the FCO information
effort. Neither really understood each other properly. The
FCO used its information budget in support of the
government's policies and specific measures; and the BBC
World Service needed the money for disseminating the image

of Britain as widely as possible, including its culture and, in general terms, 'what it stood for'. The BBC World Service operated in nearly 40 languages as well as the World Service in English, and more recently, a service in English which began at midnight and ended when the normal BBC services resumed in the early morning.

There were endless rows about who should pay what, and for what purpose. The World Service, defending its interests, often displayed a capacity for belligerence which I always felt to be at odds with its civilised, knowledgeable and cultivated staff. In short, the Foreign Office and the BBC World Service had totally different roles to perform, both in the national interest but both in a sense incompatible with each other. The World Service, at its worst, tended to think that it had the answer to the world's problems, which was to disseminate its interpretation of British interests and influence as widely as possible and to spread 'Britishness' to as many countries as it could. There was a mutual ignorance on both sides, and neglect. The FCO, for its part, let the World Service go its own way as far as they could, and was never disposed to intervene unless there were complaints from foreign governments that the World Service (in the vernacular versions, especially the Arabic Service) was getting the message wrong and damaging their interests.

Between the two of them there was much cause for quarrelling and dissent, and this was made worse by the fact that the two BBC services (the main BBC and the World Service) had tended to grow apart with the years, and the World Service people tended to regard themselves as a separate specialist corps, especially during the time of the Cold War, when many of the people at the World Service, exiled from their own countries, looked on themselves as having a propaganda role which was not shared by the fiercely independent main body of the BBC. So there were the seeds of unhappiness already planted, and much of my time was spent trying to smooth out the difficulties between the two, and of course the Foreign Office also. The Governors were a distinguished cross-section of the great and good, from all sorts of backgrounds. But on the whole, they took little detailed interest in the World Service, concentrating their efforts on the Home Services and their administration.

The Governors changed a lot during my time there. There was P.D. James, the successful crime novelist, Jane Glover, the conductor, Gwyn Jones ('Jones the Busy') of the Welsh Development Corporation, the Reverend Norman Drummond, the ex-headmaster of Loretto School, Sir Kenneth Bloomfield, the clever and experienced ex-head of the Northern Ireland Civil Service, Keith Cotes, managing director of Marks and Spencer, Joel (Lord) Barnett, ex-Financial Secretary to the previous Labour Government and, of course, Marmaduke Hussey, the Chairman, whose career had been spent mostly in newspapers and charities, the Royal Marsden Hospital being perhaps the most important of the latter. The Governors got on well together, were good judges of people, and all had rather similar views of how to reform a BBC which was old-fashioned and, in some respects, badly needed to be changed.

The BBC was lucky to have the services of 'Duke' Hussey and John Birt, with their qualities of leadership and their near-identical views and vision of the BBC's future. Having started as firm allies, however, their relationship weakened rapidly and went sharply downhill, and there was a serious clash of personalities in which the Governors could hardly fail to get involved. Indeed, the history of the final years of my time with the BBC is largely a story of attempting to patch up the worsening relationship between the Chairman and Director General which, had efforts not been made in this direction, could have broken up the Corporation altogether and done immense damage to British interests.

Rather like the Foreign Office, with which I was perhaps

196

naturally quick to compare it, the BBC had the defect of a certain inward-looking tendency: the real world was somehow theirs, in Broadcasting House, and the world outside lacked substance and reality. But there was rich talent in the organisation, as there was also in the World Service, despite the periodical violence of changes in its organisation. The latter never failed to live up to its reputation, especially abroad, as it moved closer to the BBC proper – which was, of course, one of the objects of Birt's and Hussey's reform. In the past, senior officials moved occasionally, but rarely, from one organisation to the other. There was a growing tendency for the two outfits to develop independent centres of influence. John Birt recognised this and reorganised the structure to rectify it at the cost of a public row stirred up by the World Service and its powerful supporting lobby, whose understanding of the purpose of the service seemed sometimes stuck in the war years, and even before that. Not everyone in the country, particularly those over a certain age, understood that without its close links to the main BBC, it would eventually lose all its clout.

The key to this and other problems, in my experience, was the relationship between Dukie and John. The first Governors' meeting I attended was a dinner, the object of which was to discuss and choose the Director General to succeed Michael Checkland, who had been appointed after the swift and brutal dismissal by Duke Hussey of Alistair Milne. It was an awful meeting, a majority of the Governors wishing Birt to become Director General (I certainly wanted to see this happen, as I thought the importance of the relationship between Chairman and Director General was paramount). At the meeting, Dukey and Joel Barnett, who formed a strong alliance when they agreed on things, which they mostly did, got the rest of the Governors to agree to John's appointment. The rest of the Governors did not all like this, largely because they felt they had been dragged

197

into something about which they had been insufficiently consulted. One Governor flounced out, but there was also a more fundamental difference. John Birt, the shy and studious boy from Liverpool, had the highest office in broadcasting in his hands. Educated by the Christian Fathers in working-class Liverpool, he possessed profound analytical powers and a clear idea of what he wanted. Dukie Hussey, from a completely different class background (his wife was lady-in-waiting to the Queen), wanted roughly the same things for the BBC and had a similar vision of the reforms that were necessary. They were both modernisers. The main problem between them was, as I saw it, twofold. First, while both wanted to modernise the BBC and its structure, John wanted to do so more radically and quickly than Dukie. The second was a genuine clash of personalities between the two, partly on class grounds and partly because of the very different styles of each.

The Governors for their part had little power to influence matters, rather like the Cabinet if the Prime Minister and the Chancellor of the Exchequer are determined upon a single course. There were endless committees and meetings. When I joined the BBC, I was told that it was a question of a morning's meeting once a month. Before I left the BBC, some six years later, I was a member of the Governors' Audit Committee, the Complaints Appeal Committee, the Fair Trading Committee, the Commercial Committee (Chairman), and various other Committees connected with the World Service, plus quite a few more that I cannot now remember. It all added up to about three days' work a week of intellectual effort, added to the mountains of paper which the Governors were expected to absorb (the BBC, the great communicator, seemed incapable of producing short and readable papers, and its general prose style seemed modelled on that of McKinsey & Co in its opacity).

The key person in the organisation was in my view the

Secretary of the BBC, a young man (in his thirties) called Michael Stevenson, whose job it was to look after the relationship between the Chairman and Governors and the remaining hierarchy and see that they all stuck together. I worked with Michael closely and found him a man of immense tact, intellect and humour who got on with everyone. If he sticks to his job in the BBC he will one day be Director General, if he wants to be.

I served under two chairmen – Dukie Hussey, who was an old friend, and Christopher Bland – both men of different style, but both tough in their own ways and both, when it suited them, tough on their own Governors, and not averse to criticism of their own organisation. Dukie was a subtle operator, likeable and informal. You would walk past his office (the door was always open) and he would say, 'Come in, old cock, have a glass of wine.' You would have this with him and accompany it with agreeable gossip about the work of the corporation and the people in it. Each side – you and the Chairman – would learn something from these exchanges. John Birt, easily the more knowledgeable of the two on broadcasting, was by comparison a shy and introverted person, and not the sort of man into whose office you could breeze for a minute or two without warning. Both were men of exceptional bravery. Dukie's war with the Guards cost him a leg and nearly his life at Anzio in Italy, leaving him in constant pain. John's courage, more of a moral nature, enabled him to stand firm in the face of an extraordinary storm of public vilification, especially from the traditionalists – the 'old BBC' – and their many supporters. But John never weakened and rarely even complained.

The climax of Dukie and John's deteriorating relationship came with the BBC's interview with the Princess of Wales about the breakdown in her marriage, of which Dukie (his wife being the Queen's lady-in-waiting and close friend) had no warning. People around John (perhaps even Dukie himself) obviously felt that if he had known in advance, he might have taken action to stop the programme with far-reaching results for the monarchy, the press, the public and perhaps even the existence of the BBC itself. My own small but busy part of all this was to seek to maintain the objective of keeping the BBC on the rails, aiding wherever I could the courageous and able Michael Stevenson, whose objective was the same. Dukie and John had, incredibly, not been on speaking terms for some time when the interview with the Princess of Wales took place.

John and Dukie's big achievement was the introduction of 'Producer Choice', or an internal market in the BBC, which for the first time in its history enabled the corporation to calculate what a programme would cost and encourage producers to make the best deal they could at the cheapest price. It set off a campaign of whingeing scarcely seen before even in the history of the BBC, but Hussey and Birt stuck to their guns and won the battle. Many further reforms followed, including that of the role of the Governors, who were now given a bit more clout to become a body which had some real authority and some supervising powers over the organisation in general.

There is not a lot more I can say about the BBC without going on for ever. It has undergone substantial change since the years I first became a Governor, and its organisation is crisper than it has ever been before, and its methods of working have been tightened considerably. It is to Dukie's credit that the Governors and Directors of the new BBC now all meet together in the morning once a month. Previously they had met separately, each Director being called in by the Governors to give an account of his activities during the past month. This did nothing for relations between the two bodies.

There are many people in the BBC whose names I have not yet mentioned: David Hatch, the Director of Radio when

200

I arrived there, one of the funniest men I have ever met; Will Wyatt, the cool and super-competent Director of Television; Alan Yentob, whose creative mind was responsible for many of the BBC's masterpieces in the last few years; and Ron Neil, the tough but friendly Head of Regional Broadcasting. I would be disguising the truth if I said that it was forever a happy organisation. It was always defending itself against someone – perhaps the government or government ministers, perhaps the press, and perhaps the general public who had doubts about the quality of its programmes. But I can honestly say now that the quality of its programmes and production generally has improved, and that it is still the finest general broadcasting organisation in the world. It was, however, a hard grind, especially for those – like the majority of Governors – who had no previous experience of broadcasting. I do not know what the BBC's future will be. With the multiplicity of channels now available to the general public, and the extremely wide choice available to them, the BBC's future could go either way. My hope, and that of the other Governors, is, I know, that it should continue to maintain the high standards of probity, independence, and integrity that it has always displayed in the past. We shall see.

I sprang into prominence, even notoriety, at the BBC for a few days during my third year as a Governor, when I was asked if I would go and represent the BBC in Edinburgh at the Television Festival. This is a yearly event attended by a very great many television and radio journalists. There are serious discussions and debates, and it is also a great excuse for a party. Much alcohol is consumed.

I went there because Kenneth Bloomfield, my experienced, wise and wily colleague who had been head of the Northern Ireland Civil Service, had been bitten by a bug of some kind a couple of days before and had fallen ill – too ill to get himself to Edinburgh and make a speech. It was the first time that a Governor had ever attended one of these Edinburgh conferences, and that attracted a certain attention from the media. When the time came for my appearance, I appeared on a platform with two of the senior BBC hierarchy, Jonathan Powell and Alan Yentob, both highly capable, intelligent and experienced broadcasters whose job it was to explain the changes and reforms starting to take place at the BBC and answer any questions – mostly hostile ones – from the audience, which must have numbered nearly a hundred people, some of them experts in broadcasting but the majority broadcasting journalists from all over the country. Janet Street-Porter and Howell James, two of the most amiable and entertaining people on the senior staff of the BBC, were also there and that raised my morale. The only comment on my speech when I read the draft aloud came from Jonathan Powell, who asked me if I did not have a black shirt anywhere as that seemed to be what everyone else in the audience and on the platform was wearing. I didn't, and the proceedings got under way, Powell speaking first and Yentob second, doing their best to defend the changes of the BBC while remaining loyal to Hussey and Birt, who were already much criticised figures on the part of the broadcasting community and needed strong men to come to their defence.

Their time over, I started on my own speech, which was largely confined to who the Governors were, what they did, whether they had a real job to do or not, and how they did their best to keep the BBC the kind of organisation which was traditionally admired in Britain. I finally got to the end of my speech and faced the hostile questioning. This came not so much from broadcasting experts but from broadcasting journalists who used their questions and my answers for their copy in the next day's newspapers. The BBC people at the conference, and there were very many of these, generally asked questions I could deal with and the general opinion was that I had carried out my duties very well if not absolutely brilliantly. Dukie Hussey sent a bottle of champagne to my hotel, a typically thoughtful move, and I remember drinking this or most of it after the speech had been made. The speech was really a riposte to the mischievous one made the day before by Michael Grade (who, I suspect, coveted the Chairmanship and now has it). He had occupied various senior positions at the BBC until very recently and had made assertions which were hotly challenged by the Chairman, in whose name I was speaking. Anyway, the publicity I got in the broadsheets was massive. I do not think this was really justified. I had said little that was new or surprising for the audience. However, there was a feeling among broadcasting journalists that I was a kind of Governors' spokesman. Up till then, Governors had rarely appeared in public and only very occasionally said anything of any interest.

On the way home from Edinburgh by air, I slept most of the way having had little the night before because of writing my speech. When I finally returned to our house in Sussex, my son Anthony was thrilled. 'Dad,' he said, 'you are now officially a celeb.' Despite my somewhat dubious star status, I returned to the humdrum life of a Governor, and Kenneth Bloomfield recovered from his infection, I suspect rather relieved that I had spared him what was on the whole a terrifying experience. Maggie Smith, one of the best broadcasting correspondents at that time, said she felt sorry for me, I looked so terrified – but my confidence returned as I warmed to my message, and Anne Robinson, in the chair, said some complimentary things without a trace of the rudeness she customarily displays in her own TV programme 'The Weakest Link'.

24

Other ad hoc duties, including The Red Cross, UNESCO and Prince Samy

As part of my role as the 'odds and ends' under-secretary in the 1980s, I led our delegations to Red Cross conferences, usually in Paris or Geneva. I admired the intellectual rigour, toughness and lack of sentimentality of the small group of Swiss businessmen who effectively ran it. The Foreign Office's objective was less concerned with its humanitarian work than its politicisation at the hands of the Communists, who sought to entangle it in resolutions condemning racism, anti-Semitism, colonialism and other causes which they affected to espouse, if possible in alliance with developing but non-democratic nations. The West stuck together well, and we saw them off. Meanwhile, the proper work of the Red Cross, in which the British Red Cross Society played an active, non-political role, went ahead as usual.

I also must mention my involvement with UNESCO (United Nations Educational, Scientific and Cultural Organisation), a UN subsidiary organisation without purpose or drive, but plenty of money, obsessed with producing reams of paper, which was largely ignored by its membership. I attended a number of its conferences in the eighties. The Overseas Development Agency (ODA), which was technically responsible for UNESCO in Whitehall, was quite useless in its role. Two of us from the Foreign Office were brought in to stiffen them up – particularly over a phenomenon called

204

the 'New World Information Order', enthusiastically sponsored by the Russians together with such sympathetic help as they could get from the Developing World, the objective being to pass resolutions muzzling freedom of information and giving governments control over press, radio and TV. Again, the West (with disorganised and wobbly American support) won the field.

The Sengalese chairman, Mbo, was by any standards a semi-literate crook, and his personal staff not much better. But my lasting impression is of Mbo's Number 2, an otherwise amiable Indonesian, who delivered the closing address at their general conference. I timed it: it lasted about 45 minutes and contained no substance or content whatsoever. The British press, worried and angry at first (particularly at the supine performance of the ODA), became stalwart in defeating Communist wiles and unlikely allies of the Foreign Office. The New World Information Order sank without a trace shortly afterwards. UNESCO's modest successes were over the Abu Simnel project on the Nile, and small literacy programmes in developing countries, but otherwise it was a ramp or boondoggle, costing millions of dollars and producing tons of meaningless paper in different languages to no one's benefit.

One of the more extraordinary and memorable 'odds and ends' was chairing a committee set up to find Mark Thatcher, lost during a car rally somewhere in the Sahara Desert. We kept existence of our little search party a secret from Mrs Thatcher, who would not, we knew, have approved of government money being spent on what was essentially a private matter, despite her being worried about her missing son. Eventually his father, Denis, tracked him down, not particularly grateful for having been found and saved.

The most spectacular of these many ad hoc jobs, however, involved a Turkish gentleman called Prince Samy, a minor member of what was then the Iraqi royal family. He was also a fairly substantial shareholder in the Iraq Petroleum Corporation. At one point it became necessary for him to flee Turkey, and this he did with at least 20 family members, on board a British warship As so often happens, the debt Samy owed the British became in his mind and that of others a debt we owed him. He was settled in London in rented accommodation in Chapel Street, W1, and was paid an annual stipend found somewhere and somehow by the government of the day. He invariably used this up in a few months and was constantly on the telephone to the private secretary to the head of the Foreign Office asking for more. Eventually, the latter decided that enough was enough and paid him a fairly substantial lump sum to get him off our backs. This was unwise, as Samy spent it all in a matter of weeks and insisted on more. One of our problems was that he had three powerful backers – Lord Hailsham, the Lord Chancellor, whose judgement was by then erratic, Julian Amery MP, who found some mad political reason for coming to his aid, and Commander Marten, a landowner who fought and won, after the war, a battle over his large estate at Crichel in Dorset which the Ministry of Defence had appropriated.

Samy was passed from private secretary to private secretary. There was much reluctance to take on his case. He was a dapper little man, who spoke English with an upper-class accent. His shoes, always exquisitely polished, were hand-made by Lobb, and suits by the best tailors in Saville Row, and he was invariably polite, though not above blackmail. No one else in the Foreign Office would take him on. He was insistent that he had done us some service in the Middle East, probably of a secret nature, and we therefore owed him a pension for life. None of us had time to investigate this, and as is usual in such cases, there appeared to be no files. I think I got the worst side of Samy. A couple of times he telephoned me to announce that he would shoot himself – indeed, he said he had a revolver in his hand as we spoke. 'I wouldn't do that, Prince Samy,' I replied nervously. Then, even worse, when evicted from his house, he threatened to camp with his family in the Foreign Office courtyard unless we gave him more money. His family consisted of a number of old and veiled ladies (aunts?), some younger men (cousins?), who were not quite right in the head, and some menials who, I suppose, pressed his suits and polished the Lobb shoes.

The implications of the family living (and cooking) in the Foreign Office courtyard and resisting eviction was an unattractive one, and I thought I had better report the whole business to Sir Geoffrey Harrison, who was in charge of the Office in Harold Caccia's absence somewhere. Geoffrey Harrison was as keen as everyone else in the Office not to get involved, and my release from Samy only came when I was not long afterwards sent to another post. My lasting memory of Samy is that he divided his Foreign Office contacts into (as it were) gentlemen and players. I was definitely a gentleman, so was Douglas Hurd. I am not so sure about the status of John Ford or Robert Wade-Gery. Patrick Wright was not himself sure whether he belonged to one group or the other.

Afterword

It is not easy to summarise such a mixture of experiences and anecdotes with serious reflections. I can best do this, perhaps, by quoting the words of Clem Conger, Assistant Chief of Protocol in the State Department in Washington. 'Goodbye, Nick,' he said, as we parted after working closely together for four years. 'It's been real.'